Teleportation!
A Practical Guide
For The Metaphysical Traveler

Teleportation!

A Practical Guide
for the Metaphysical Traveler

Gwen Totterdale, Ph.D.
Jessica Severn, Ph.D.

Words of Wizdom International, Inc.
Miami Beach, Florida

Printed in the United States of America

First Printing January 1996

ISBN: 1-884695-42-6

Library of Congress Cataloging-In-Publication Data

Totterdale, Gwen, 1952-
    Teleportation! : a practical guide for the metaphysical traveler /
by Gwen Totterdale, Jessica Severn.
        p.   cm.
    Includes bibliographical references.
    ISBN 1-884695-42-6 (softcover)
    1. Teleportation.   I. Severn, Jessica June Hattie. II. Title.
BF1386.T68   1995
133.8--dc20   95-38954
                                                              CIP

ACKNOWLEDGEMENTS

The publisher and authors wish to express special thanks to the following individuals, copyright holders, publishers and organizations:

Fredric Lehrman, Director of Nomad University, who is perpetually travelling, both physically and metaphysically, for permission to quote from *The Sacred Landscape;*

Robert V. Gerard and Oughten House Publications, P.O. Box 2008, Livermore, California 94551-2008, USA, for permission to quote from *The Crystal Stair,* by Eric Klein;

Hedda Lark and DeVorss & Co., for permission to quote from Volume 3, page 46, *Life and Teachings of the Masters of The Far East,* by Baird T. Spalding;

Crown Publishers Inc. for permission to quote from *Ageless Body, Timeless Mind*, by Deepak Chopra;

Penguin USA for permission to quote from *Sydney Omarr's Astrological Guide...,1995/Scorpio* by Sydney Omarr, Copyright © 1994 by Sydney Omarr. Used by permission of Dutton Signet, a division of Penguin Books USA Inc.;

HarperCollins Publishers and Dr. Wayne W. Dyer, for permission to quote selected quotations from *Real Magic: Creating Miracles In Everyday Life* by Dr. Wayne W. Dyer;

The Miami Herald, for permission to reprint the entire article, *"The Lore and Legend of Bimini,"* by Fred Tasker, and to Fred Tasker for writing such an interesting article;

Bantam Books, a division of Bantam Doubleday Dell Publishing Group, Inc. for permission to reprint from *Emmanuel's Book* by Pat Rodegast and Judith Stanton. Copyright (c) 1985 by Pat Rodegast;

Richard Bach, for his inspirational writings in *Jonathan Livingston Seagull.*

***The philosophy of one century
is the common sense of the next.***

- Chinese Fortune Cookie

Table of Contents

PREFACE

There is a lot of talk about paradigms these days. Shifting, changing, bending paradigms. Paradigms are simply collections of beliefs, values and ideas that, bundled together, create models for what groups of people believe. Today, many cultures share paradigms on a large number of subjects. Most people, for example, share the belief that humans are born, grow older and then die. (The paradigm around what happens after death depends, in great part, on particular religious belief systems.)

Many of the major belief systems that have been collectively supported, however, are changing. Some are changing quickly, dramatically. The business arena, for example, sports several new books radically challenging *the old way of doing business.* The authors of these books state several reasons business must change, citing trends toward global marketing, changes within the family structure, emerging political systems, changing demographics and shifting economic bases. However, perhaps the major element leading to change in the way the world conducts business is the *change in the way that people think.*

And it's not just business that is undergoing massive paradigm shifts. The same holds true for communication, technology, transportation, health care and education. United States President Bill Clinton based his entire campaign on the concept of change, a different way of living.

People in America, and in many parts of the world, are ushering in a new era. Ready or not, the times are truly changing.

What better time, then, to consider the nature of individual reality? Quantum physicists explain that time and space, as they have been defined, really don't exist except as a concept, a framework. Many go on to describe the human body as simply a pulse, a vibration that holds certain elements together through each individual's unique DNA. Simply put, individual consciousness is energy holding physical matter together. Is it possible, even advantageous, to move forward now with these new perceptions of the nature of human beings?

Humans have more potential than ever before imagined, much of it lying latent in physical bodies. Human abilities are waiting to be expressed! Scientists and researchers in numerous fields are exploring the range of human potential, questioning and often quickly erasing the limits that have long been held up as truths about physical reality.

Human minds, individually and collectively, are amazingly powerful. This mental energy can be directed to exceed many of the limits within which we have been operating.

WHY WE WROTE THIS BOOK

This is why we collaborated on this book about teleportation. We wanted to move beyond limiting belief systems. We wanted to explore new realms of consciousness and share our results with others. We wanted to bring to light new methods of travel, communication and connecting. And we wanted to assist in activating those parts within us, and *you*, that want to grow.

Sydney Omarr, the highly regarded U.S. astrologer, discusses the significance of our planet's movement beginning in 1995, a year of *breakthroughs:*

> *The year 1995 marks the beginning of an era of incredible global mobility. While some may choose to stay home and log onto a world communication network, others may investigate the new possibilities in long-distance travel, such as high-speed trains and planes, solar-powered vehicles, and many high-tech advances in automobiles. Individual mobility also takes new leaps.*

He goes on to discuss the major significance of this time period, as we move toward the new millennium:

> *On a deeper, evolutionary level, this is a time when those who have strongly held, in-*

flexible beliefs and principles may realize that there are many different points of view that are equally valid. Over the past few years, there has been much dissolution of the boundaries between cultures, and now the actual cross-contact will begin, thanks to global media and new trade agreements.

... Thanks to the new global society, there will be much more exposure to other cultures, and mutual exchange of ideas and beliefs. And through these exchanges, we should be able to arrive at a more universal understanding and tolerance of each other's version of truth.

True, there will be many who will not want to risk their safe, established belief systems, or who will fiercely resist any challenges, as happened during the Spanish Inquisition. But the most positive way to use this transit is through an attitude of mutual sharing, realizing that differing belief systems have valuable insights to why we are here. By exposure to many diverse points of view through the new globalism of Pluto in Sagittarius, we should have a much better understanding of who we are as a world culture and what our higher purpose might be.

...And by confronting our own belief systems, we should come closer to discovering an authentic individual personal truth for ourselves. Many of us will be shaken up and transformed; however, in doing so, we may also have a true experience of a higher power. *

We agree, and we are excited about the prospects! Welcome to the new paradigm on metaphysical travel!

Gwen Totterdale, Ph.D.
The Island of O'ahu, Hawaii 1995

Jessica Severn, Ph.D.
Camano Island, Washington 1995

*From SYDNEY OMARR'S ASTROLOGICAL GUIDE...,1995/ SCORPIO by Sydney Omarr. Copyright (c) 1994 by Sydney Omarr. Used by permission of Dutton Signet, a division of Penguin Books USA Inc.

Chapter One

PERFECT SPEED IS BEING THERE

Jonathan Livingston Seagull was quite a gull. Jonathan spent most of his life learning to fly — not to *just* fly, but to *really* fly. Jonathan learned to move around at great speeds, with acrobatic timing and performance. He flew in a way few gulls had ever even considered flying before.

His story, in the globally best-selling tale ***Jonathan Livingston Seagull*** by Richard Bach, is one of adventure, courage, motivation, trust and magic. Jonathan became so accomplished with flight that he began to move to new levels, getting a glimpse, literally, into new ways of flying. One day, in fact, Jonathan happened upon the "world" of teleportation...

BACKGROUND

Jonathan Livingston Seagull had been cast out of his

flock because he refused to give up his one love in life —
flying — and to behave as the other gulls did. Spending his
days and nights alone, then, his learning accelerated as rapidly as his flying speed! Jonathan was happy.

One day he was visited by two *other-worldly* gulls
who took him to a new level, to another school of learning.
Jonathan mistakenly thought he was in Heaven, for he began to glow as brightly as the gulls who were escorting him.
And he was — finally — among gulls of like mind, gulls who
loved to fly as he did!

AND THEN CAME...

After a time Jonathan approached an Elder gull,
Chiang, to ask what was going on and if, indeed, he had
entered Heaven. Chiang imparted the kind of universal
wisdom that teachers give to their students — when, of
course, the students are ready. Chiang told Jonathan he
was not in Heaven, because Heaven is not a place. It is a
state of mind. Specifically, a *perfect* state of mind. To demonstrate his point, Chiang performed the unimaginable: he
willed his body to disappear, only to appear in an instant
many yards away! Then he reversed his direction, returning to his original spot next to Jonathan.

He defied what we consider the physical laws of nature, for he moved without physical effort, crossing over
measurable space and back, all within the blink of an eye.
Chiang was demonstrating through his actions that Heaven

was only a *perfect* thought away!

"*It's kind of fun,*" [1] Chiang mused.

Want to learn to touch Heaven?
We thought so. Read on....

Teleportation!

Chapter Two

TELEPORTATION: WHAT IS IT?

Let us not ask 'what is it?'
Let us go and make our visit.

T.S. Elliot

You can explore the movement of your body
without physical movement.
You can explore the concept of teleportation.
You can explore how to be unlimited while in a physical body.

MARKAS

So just what *is* Jonathan Livingston Seagull's teacher doing as he disappears, only to reappear almost instantaneously in a different location? What is the dynamic being observed? This is an example of teleportation.

Teleportation is the process of physically relocating one's body to another place *without* physical movement and then, usually, returning to the original departure point. The art of teleportation is more than theory-based. And it lies beyond the fanciful imaginings of sci-fi enthusiasts. It springs from a well of ancient knowledge that encourages expansion and exploration. To go anywhere at a moment's thought, *"you must begin by knowing you have already arrived,"*[2] knowing you can expand your world, explore new sights. From this state of expansion you can begin to choose more and more resources to help you on your path.

What we are describing here, in a teleportation experience, is that the physical body dematerializes (disappears) from one spot and then rematerializes (appears) in a different place in an instant. It's an experience similar to Star Trek's "Beam me up, Scottie," but without the use of the transporter!

Teleportation is not a new concept. It's been around for a long, long time. In a five volume classic from the metaphysical literature, *Life and Teaching of the Masters of the Far East*, author and explorer Baird T. Spalding describes how he personally witnessed teleportation by the masters of the Far East. Spalding also describes, in Volume Three, how one of the members of his party learned to teleport after observing how the masters seemed to appear and disappear at will. Feeling frustrated about recent experiences his team had been through, Spalding listened to a member describe his disheartening feeling after observing a human act of terrorism against fellow humans:

> *"Every one of us has taken upon himself*
> *the condition of the experience through which*

we have passed. This is what is now hamper-
ing us and I for one am through with that thing,
it is no part of me whatsoever. It is not mine
only as I worship it and hold to it and do not
let it go. I step forth out of this condition into a
higher and better condition and let go. I am
entirely through with it." As we stood and
stared at him (Spalding reported), we realized
he was gone, he had disappeared. [3]

A present day example of teleportation is repeatedly demonstrated by Sai Baba, a well-known Hindu master, who can transport his physical body from the bottom of a long hill to the top instantaneously. This phenomenon has been witnessed by large crowds of people — followers and skeptics alike.

In the United States greater numbers of people, mainstream and otherwise, are considering the possibilities associated with energy transformation. For example, an article in the September 20, 1994 *Wall Street Journal*, "Research Institute Shows People a Way Out of Their Bodies," describes the many participants seeking out-of-body experiences at the Monroe Institute in Virginia. From the ranks of industry, military, and service professionals, those wanting to experience an unlimited way of being and apply it in all areas of their lives have, for the past 21 years, found their way to the Monroe Institute.

And the concept of teleportation has now hit the air waves, with television series such as *Star Trek, The Next*

Generation and *The Tomorrow People,* introducing the phenomenon to millions of viewers! Even small children are aware of teleportation. A new toy called *StarTrek, The Next Generation, Teleportation Molecular Beam Transportation System* ™Playmate, allows children to "teleport" tiny figures from one play area to another!

Teleportation is unique. It is therefore important to distinguish teleportation from other phenomena that, at first glance, might seem similar. To do this, let's take a look at:

WHAT TELEPORTATION IS NOT. . .

Alchemy

Alchemy is the precursor of modern chemistry and metallurgy. The word "alchemy" comes from Greek terms meaning "to tear" and "to bring together." Physically, alchemy is the art of transmuting one base material, such as mercury, into another material, such as gold or silver. Symbolically, however, alchemy represents the transformation of consciousness.

The well-known psychiatrist Carl G. Jung had a great interest in alchemy in terms of its value for helping us to understand human psychology and behavior. He began focusing on the subject of alchemy after a prophetic dream in 1926. Jung delivered a lecture entitled, "Dream Symbols and the Individuation Process," in Switzerland in 1935 and continued to study the significance of alchemy as a symbol for transformation throughout his career.

Teleportation is not alchemy — it does not change one substance into another, either physically or symbolically. In a teleportation experience one's body moves to a different location, retaining the same physical properties after its instantaneous move.

Ascension

Ascension, as described in *The Crystal Stair: A Guide to the Ascension* by Eric Klein, is,

> *... a great leap of experience on every level of your being. In general, you could say it is a leap from third dimensional reality into a fifth dimensional or higher state of consciousness ... the fifth dimension or higher, the ascended state, is a state of increased frequency of vibration.* [4]

In some very important ways, ascension is similar to teleportation. In both cases, the individual is learning to expand his or her focus beyond the physical world as we perceive it every day. However, ascension is essentially the transmutation of the physical body into another state of being, a nonphysical state. While persons who ascend may elect to return to the physical body to assist others with the process, the basic goal is to change the state of the physical body and enter into another dimension.

Gary Bonnell, in an excellent book entitled *Ascension: The Original Teachings of Christ Awareness,* describes ascension as a teleportation process of sorts, in which individuals are able to visit other realms of consciousness by changing their energy fields into light body form. He suggests that to develop an advanced ability such as ascension, it is necessary to release belief structures that are influenced by separate thoughts and feelings. These personal beliefs are derived from mass consciousness.

This evolution of the soul — while in physical body, and in our current time/space dimension — allows movement into other dimensions in the universe.

Ascension, then, is dematerialization, similar to teleportation. But the goal of teleportation is to simply relocate the physical body to another location within this dimension. And while the body does change physical locations for a short period of time, it usually returns, intact, to its original "take off" point when a particular teleportation experience is complete.

Another difference between ascension and teleportation is that the focus of ascension seems to be primarily a *spiritual* activity, in that the objective is to move into an etheric realm of consciousness; teleportation, on the other hand, is more *mental* in nature, using mind over matter to reconstruct one's physical reality. In both activities however, a greater portion of the brain is utilized than is generally the case in day to day living. Part of the process, and one of the goals of both activities, is learning to awaken, individually, to the unlimited potential that lies just beneath the surface in each of us.

Astral Projection, Astral Travel, Soul Travel

Astral projection, also known as an out-of-body experience, normally occurs during times of deep relaxation, meditation or sleep state. Your consciousness, or soul, goes out of, beyond, your physical body. Often times this happens spontaneously. With this type of experience the conscious mind may be aware of what is occurring, but from a perspective that is different from that of the physical body, which remains passive. Many students of metaphysics have learned to do astral projection consciously, at will. Reports of this phenomenon are nearly universal and date to antiquity. Teleportation differs from these out-of-body experiences in that the entire physical body "travels" to a new location; an out-of-body experience is simply the soul traveling.

Dreaming

Random House dictionary defines a 'dream' as a succession of images, thoughts, or emotions occurring during sleep. For the most part, people are not aware that they are dreaming *as it is happening*. Sometimes, however, a person does become aware of dreaming while remaining

27

asleep; this phenomenon is called lucid dreaming. Lucid dreams are often characterized by bright colors, strong emotions and frequently, sensations of flying or levitation. As the individual becomes aware of being in a dream, he/she will often times begin to "direct" the dream, or move the activity in the direction they want it to go.

Teleportation, like dreams, can also occur during sleep state. It differs from both typical dreams and lucid dreams, however, in that the teleporter's body physically leaves the bed. If someone were to be watching as teleportation took place, for example, the experience of the sleeping person beginning to dematerialize would occur. We will discuss this type of teleportation more in Chapter Six.

Levitation

Levitation has been described as an experience in which a person or object rises up and floats in mid-air. As with many of the phenomena we have been discussing, the concept and practice of levitation dates back to ancient times. Cases of levitation have been reported throughout the world and across many different religious, philosophical and cultural perspectives. Views on what this activity represents range from a holy, sacred activity to one of demonic possession, depending on the cultural bias of those observing the phenomena.

With the experience of levitation the physical body does not dematerialize but rather floats upward — intact

— in basically one area. Teleportation means the physical body dematerializes and rematerializes in another location. The body doesn't simply "hang out" above the ground in the same place, but travels to different places.

Remote Viewing

Remote viewing, which is defined as the seeing and sensing of distant places or objects clairvoyantly, has been reported as early as 550 B.C. Ancient Greek and Roman leaders consulted oracles when they needed help making important decisions. The most famous of these oracles were the priestesses at Delphi who were said to use remote viewing to find the answers to seekers' questions. Shamans, priests, healers and seers from Tibet to Siberia, Africa to the Americas, have used one form or another of remote viewing in the course of their work. Soviet, American and Canadian governments have conducted extensive research on the subject as have academic researchers such as the major research efforts currently being carried out at Princeton University. [5]

When a person has a remote viewing experience, a distant object or place is viewed with the "psychic" eye, i.e. in the mind only. In a teleportation experience, however, a distant object or place is physically visited, so that everything is viewed with physical eyes, on location.

Telepathy

Telepathy, often referred to as mental telepathy or "telepathic communication" is the mind to mind transference of thoughts and emotions between two individuals or among animals. Derived from the Greek terms "tele" (distant) and "pathe" (occurrence or feeling), the practice of telepathy spans the globe and has also been described since very early times. Sigmund Freud addressed the phenomenon as:

> *a regressive, primitive faculty lost in the course of evolution, but which still had the ability to manifest under certain conditions.*[6]

Psychiatrist Carl G. Jung took the phenomenon of telepathy very seriously as did American psychologist and philosopher William James, who encouraged further research of this experience. In 1971 the Apollo 14 astronaut Edgar D. Mitchell conducted an unauthorized experiment in telepathy with four subjects on earth — 150,000 miles away. His results, reported after the mission was completed, were moderately significant. Telepathy involves the sending out of ideas and emotions to another person or place, much like sending a mental "letter." Teleportation, again, refers to the actual physical relocation of one's body.

Telekinesis

Telekinesis is defined as the causing of an object to move by unexplainable means, as by the mind. It is similar to teleportation in that it is a mental activity, but the object being "moved" is outside and independent of the physical body. In telekinesis, one is causing objects to move, not one-self.

From these descriptions of various phenomena, you can see that while each is quite remarkable, they are all different from the teleportation experience. What, then, *is* a teleportation experience?

WHAT TELEPORTATION LOOKS LIKE

If you are watching one or more friends during the teleportation process, it will appear that they, or parts of them, literally fade from view: it is similar to a "fade out" on a movie screen. The rest of your surroundings remains the same. From your perspective your friends appear to slowly dissipate from your physical reality.

If *you* are the teleporter, on the other hand, you will experience several things simultaneously. First, you will feel your energy vibrating at an increasing rate. Often times there will be the sensation of your energy spiraling upwards, and your physical body feels a tingling, buzzing sensation.

31

As the energy moves you may feel a kind of "pop" coming out of the top of your head. And if your eyes are open, you will see a new "scenario" filling in around you as you leave your old environment behind.

Learning to teleport can be compared to the initial stages of learning to ride a bicycle. First you get on and begin peddling as fast as you can. If you're lucky, you will travel several yards before falling over. Somewhat frustrated, you nevertheless decide you really want to master riding a bicycle because it is a new "freedom machine," and because it feels good! So you get back on it and try again. And again. And again. And as you practice and develop your skills, you begin to stay up on the bicycle for longer periods of time.

The same process happens in teleportation. You set up practice sessions, mentally sensing your energy over and over until you feel that first "pop," which indicates a tangible shift in your body's energy. How to do this will be described in detail in Chapter Five. Even though you will have to practice to develop and refine your skills, from the first "pop" you are a member of the teleportation club! And from that point forward all you need to do is practice, practice, practice. Richard Bach once wrote that the difference between the amateur and the professional writer is that a professional just keeps writing.

Practice is the key to becoming an experienced teleporter!

This is teleportation in its simplest form. In the next few chapters we'll be discussing the wheres, whens and hows of teleportation techniques. But perhaps the best way to summarize this concept right here is to say,

Now you see me............ now you don't!

Teleportation!

Chapter Three

WHY DO IT?

When you sit in a spot, your energy becomes saturated
with the tone of the place. Imagine a teabag that had
no flavor, color, or properties of its own,
but only absorbed the qualities around it.
Let yourself sit until you are done.
Fredric Lehrman,
The Sacred Landscape

There comes a time when the mind takes a higher plane
of knowledge but can never prove how it got there.
All great discoveries have involved such a leap.
The important thing is not to stop questioning.
Albert Einstein

Why in the world would anyone want to learn to
teleport? The only way we know to answer this question is
with another question: Why do you choose to learn anything that you do? Probably for any number of reasons.
What is your motivation for developing skills in some areas, while letting other opportunities go by? For some, they
wish to learn teleportation because they want to find a faster
means of travel. For others, it may be that they enjoy the
mysteries of paranormal experiences.

Some of you may view it as another step on your path to psychic development or spiritual enlightenment. For example, developing new light bodies is a path many take as they expand their spiritual awareness. And for some it might be the proverbial response of the mountain climber: *Because it's there!*

The reasons why someone, anyone, would want to develop in this area will be as unique to the individuals and their past experiences as the individuals themselves. But if you go within, if you take a look at the deeper aspects of who you are, you will find the common denominator of motivation among all of us: *energy expansion.* Just as the creation of the universe came about because of the desire for expansion, i.e. growth, so do our desires in our own personal universes reflect this cause-and-effect scenario. The soul has a craving to go beyond what it knows consciously now, what it has already mastered. Souls, our souls, want to express themselves. And for some — what we believe will become true for more and more people — one of the ways of expanding their energies will be through the practice of teleportation.

MIND OVER MATTER

The idea of mind over matter has been brought to light when describing many incredible situations. For example, some people have willed themselves to recover from a serious illness. Others have moved themselves to new physical feats, such as faster times in a race, endurance in weightlifting and lifting heavy items, in dire situations, from persons pinned underneath. Through visualization, some people are able to bring great surges in their business activities. The use of one's mental abilities in a conscious fashion can, and will, bring about changes in status, profession, family ties, prosperity — for, as the saying goes:

Anything you perceive, you can achieve.

Those who have participated in our teleportation classes and seminars have shared some of their personal motivations surrounding teleportation:

> *I'm not sure (why I want to learn to teleport). It's something that's a compulsion within me, and I don't know entirely on a conscious level why. I want to be able to reconnect with what I somehow know I can do. I want to remember. Sometimes I hope I can do it. Other times I know I can do it.* Question: How can you shift from "I think I can" to "I know I can?" *By being there already.*

> *I think for me the dematerializing and materializing would be the ultimate of the power of mind over matter, and I think that's why I'm interested in teleportation. And with what you said about the dolphins (teleporting to be with them), that was giving me another*

big clue about why, suddenly, I found myself interested in teleportation.

I'd like to feel that this is really happening, that it was confirmation of our power to do these things. And it just sounds so exciting, period.

It would give me a much more concrete knowing that I have mastery over my mental abilities. It makes it concrete rather than something I just imagined to be true, believed to be true, when I read about it, that the great Yogis have done it on this planet. So I'd like to do it myself. I want to be more masterful myself.

I want to do it just so I know I can do it. Just to feel I can do it. I believe I've done it in sleep state. I do believe that. But to be aware of it, to be able to do it in waking state. And it's a means to an end, for transmigration. (See Chapter 8 for a description of transmigration.)

For fun.

CONNECTIONS WITH ATLANTIS

Many of those interested in teleportation have mentioned they feel a strong link with ancient Atlantis. Much has been written, with even more speculation in the metaphysical community, about a lost continent first mentioned by the Greek philosopher, Plato: Atlantis. It is believed by many who have investigated ancient mysteries and folklore that the Atlanteans were very advanced mentally. It is also theorized that those among the culture who were even further developed used their mental powers to teleport.

On June 17, 1990 an article entitled,*"The Lore and Legend of BIMINI,"* was printed in *The Miami Herald* (see Appendix I for full article). The waters surrounding Bimini, part of the chain of islands known as the Bahamas, were identified by Edgar Cayce as the hub of ancient Atlantis (see Chapter Seven). The article reports the following about Cayce and his predictions:

> *The seventh-grade dropout-turned 'sleeping-prophet' (1877-1945), believed he could diagnose illness, interpret dreams, read the past and foretell the future in a hypnotic trance. It was in exploring his subjects' past lives that Cayce discovered Atlantis, a topic that came to make up 30 percent of Cayce's life readings.*
>
> *His concept was even more wondrous, if a bit fuzzier, than Plato's. He believed Atlantis was an island near Bimini where an advanced civilization peaked in 50,000 B.C. and was destroyed in 10,000 B.C. By understanding the Earth's fundamental electrical and gravitational forces, Atlanteans built "boats" that flew by something akin to teleportation. The same forces helped Atlanteans lift mammoth stones to build splendid temples.* [7]

Those who feel a strong connection or perhaps have had past-life recall of living in Atlantis, may want to learn, or rediscover, teleportation in this life. In a session of automatic writing by Gwen, advice from spirit came through on the topic of teleportation. This guide, known to Gwen as Lancelot, discussed the relevance of teleportation to an upcoming trip, in 1992, to the island of Bimini (again, see Chapter Seven):

The art of teleportation is more than theory-based. It springs from a well of ancient knowledge that encourages expansion and exploration. To go anywhere at a moment's thought, you must begin by knowing you have already arrived. Then you are free to choose resources that acknowledge your wisdom rather than question it.

So what does it mean to teleport?

Can you move faster than the speed of light?
Is that important to you?

Can you climb new heights, see views you have never seen?
Is that important to you?

Can you at last live freely in a world wrought
with restrictions?
Is that important to you?

Or, can you now begin to accept the power that lies deep
within you,
power that is unlimited but to this point has not been
unrestricted?
And what of the attached responsibility?

Is this desired by you?

Why Do It?

This is why you return to Bimini, all of you.
To embrace the responsibility of power as you have,
in the past, embraced the power of Atlantis.
A humbling experience, teleportation,
because it brings to you the wisdom of the ancients
in a world that does not support such knowledge.

And it is for you to live the knowledge.
And it is for you to live the knowledge in the face of
ridicule, of those who believe in
the physical world and nothing beyond,
those that would silence you,
or disrupt the abilities you wish to express.

When it becomes more important to you to love
your process of creation,
then will you experience teleportation.

When it becomes more important to you to see
what lies beyond your line of vision,
then will you experience teleportation.

When it becomes more important to you to feel
total love and self-acceptance,
then you will begin to fly.

This truly is only the beginning.

Lancelot

OTHER MOTIVATIONS

These are just some of the thoughts and feelings expressed about one's opportunity to teleport. Many others have mentioned more practical reasons, such as traveling to visit relatives; exploring places not easily accessible by plane, boat or train; or saving on travel costs. And you can have more than one reason for your interest! Whatever your motivation, the important thing here is to be conscious of it.

And remember, to develop this skill, it is necessary to focus on your interest in it, not on trying to learn it in order to prove anything to others who are less metaphysically inclined. This is about you developing and expanding your energies! The purpose, real purpose, of teleportation is the transformation of one's energy. If you try to use it to prove something to someone, you will probably create disappointment for yourself. Why? Because not everyone wants to learn teleportation, or to follow along a path similar to yours. If your intention is to demonstrate to others that such things exist, you will be giving your power away, and it will create ongoing difficulties for you. Instead, focus on why you want to learn to teleport. Those who are interested will naturally be intrigued, without you needing to get their approval.

Deepak Chopra, in his book, *Ageless Body, Timeless Mind*, discusses the importance of learning on one's physical body:

Why Do It?

The second mode of activity engages the intricate process called learning, which is at the root of growing, as opposed to growing old... When you start to assert control over any bodily process, the effect is holistic. The mind body system reacts to every single stimulus, i.e. to stimulate one cell is to stimulate all.[8]

Use your self-motivation and desires, then, to inspire, stimulate and guide you, along with the following chapters, into a new mode of transportation!

Who dares to go where no man — or woman — has dared to go? Some sweet inspirations...

Teleportation!

Chapter Four

WHO CAN DO IT?

*A truth once seen, even by a single mind,
always ends imposing itself on the
totality of human consciousness.*
Pierre Teilhard de Chardin

**And then the mountain disappears without a trace,
And all it took was a sudden Leap of Faith.**
Kenny Loggins

In her watershed book, *The Aquarian Conspiracy*,
Marilyn Ferguson discusses the Victorian fantasy, *Flatland*,[9]
written by Edwin A. Abbot. *Flatland* is the story of a being
named Square who lived in a two dimensional world. Life
went along well for Square until one night when, in dream
state, he encountered a three dimensional being. The idea
of a third dimension began to haunt Square in his waking
life. Square began to believe in the reality of a three dimensional existence, having felt, or experienced it, in dream
state. He shared his beliefs with the other residents of
Flatland. Frightened by this new concept, an idea they could
not relate to, the Flatlanders dealt with their fear by impris-

oning Square. Square remained locked up for the rest of his life because, although he could not explain his beliefs, he could not let them go. In other words, having had the experience, he was not able to deny it.

New ideas, as they begin to challenge prevailing belief systems on an individual level, can be unnerving to both the "thinker" and those who have not yet considered these thoughts. For some the notion of changing or moving beyond the current paradigm is simply too uncomfortable. Attacking the thinker is seemingly safer than messing with the status quo. As Einstein surmised,

> *"great thinkers will always experience opposition from mediocre minds."*

The prevailing paradigm in our world today is that we live in a three dimensional reality. We are not threatened by two, or even one dimensional concepts because we've already experienced them. However, just as Square found another dimension, so, too, can we begin to explore the possibilities that lie in dimensions poised to be discovered, dimensions that seemingly lie outside of the time-space continuum.

Challenging a prevailing paradigm is not something done consciously at first — rather, it comes from the heart. It begins with the recognition that something is not quite "right" in our perspective, or that there is more here than meets the eye.

Technological change is occurring so quickly that what is new today will shortly become memories of the past. The changes we've been discussing are not so far away; in fact, some are already occurring. The reality of teleportation among the masses is fast approaching. What pragmatic form it will take in our everyday lives is yet to be seen. For some, it will remain an impossibility because they will choose not to entertain the possibility. But for those who wish to move into expanded realms of consciousness, the seeds are beginning to take root.

Unconscious beliefs, encased in limitations, can keep you from experiencing the world of teleportation. Listen to the chatter inside your head. Does it argue for limitation or does it encourage the exploration of new ideas? Becoming conscious of the beliefs that you hold is a good first step in releasing those that "hold you" back.

MOVERS AND "SHIFTERS"

Throughout history people with beliefs based in limitation have tried to discourage forward, visionary thought. Perhaps someone told Christopher Columbus, "Don't rock the boat, Chris, and leave the Queen alone!" And can't you just see a neighbor leaning on the fence, chewing a blade of grass, predicting, "It'll never fly, Wilber....."

But pioneers, adventurers with vision — like you — have dared to take risks, to explore the unknown and to follow their hearts, in spite of external criticism. Anyone who *really wants to learn* the techniques of teleportation can, *and will*. It all begins with a desire — a passion, really — to move into new realms of consciousness. And, it takes vision: the ability to see and imagine yourself beyond the present way of doing things.

There are many stories of unparalleled achievements that have inspired us through the ages to go beyond the limited ways we have perceived ourselves. Here are just a few examples of visionary thinkers.

MUSIC

John Lennon

John Lennon was born during a bombing raid in Liverpool, England on October 9, 1940. Family difficulties forced the young child to be raised with distant relatives and to be shuttled about between various schools and programs. He grew up without the love and comfort of a stable family environment.

In 1956 his Aunt Mimi bought John his first guitar. After hearing her nephew play the instrument for hours on end she later commented,

"The guitar's all very well as a hobby, John, but you'll never make a living out of it."[10]

But John continued to spend hours and hours playing his guitar, and in 1957 he teamed with Paul McCartney to join a group of young teen musicians. Only a year later, George Harrison was asked to play with John's band. By 1960 John Lennon had dropped out of college to work full-time with music.

From his first recorded song, "Hello Little Girl," recorded by the Beatles in 1962, to his final album, *Double Fantasy*, released in November, 1980, John Lennon changed music forever. Using melody and lyrics to teach, Lennon offered a new vision to listeners everywhere: peace is possible, love is really all there is, people are in control of their own lives and the power of imagination can change the world.

Around the globe young people, and eventually persons of all ages, races and creeds, began to consider, at least in part, the message of John Lennon. There is hardly a country in the world today that remains untouched by the music of the Beatles and John Lennon.

Lennon once noted that he believed in everything until it was disproved, including fairies, myths and dragons. He felt that reality left a lot to the imagination.

But the vision and forward thinking of Lennon was not always appreciated. He was jailed several times for everything from possession of marijuana to his involvement with radicals such as Jerry Rubin, Abbie Hoffman and Rennie Davis. Some of his albums were banned as being obscene, although the only "obscene elements" were photos of John and Yoko standing naked, or in love-making poses.

John Lennon had a vision of harmony, love and peace. He tried to share that vision and offer the possibility that simply reaching inward and using imagination and emotions, could indeed bring about real change in the world.

John Lennon was shot and killed in front of his home. But the essence of John Lennon is alive today. He continues to inspire and promote love, peace and gentle personal awareness through his music, lyrics and vision.

LAW

Justice Harry Blackmum

While much has been written about the famous Supreme Court Case, Roe v. Wade, it is valuable to look beyond the prosecutors and defenders in this case and to turn our attention to the justice who wrote the landmark Supreme Court decision that made abortion legal in the United States.

During one of the most controversial modern day court cases, Justice Harry Blackmum was asked to write the court's opinion. This job called for great forward vision and held tremendous responsibility. The justice was forced to consider all views with a clear and unbiased reading and to use the law to resolve moral decisions for an entire nation.

Challenged with the task, Blackmum took many months to write the opinion. During that time he was hounded from those on all sides of the issue. On more than one occasion, he publicly expressed the strain and struggle he felt from such a monumental undertaking. His fellow judges and advisors were appalled that he would allow personal feelings to leak to the public. After all, Supreme Court justices are supposed to be cool and calm and to have everything in order.

After hearing months and months of arguments on both sides of the issue, and after vast amounts of reading and study, Justice Blackmum was ready to present the views of the court.

"This right of privacy... is broad enough to encompass a woman's decision whether or not to terminate her pregnancy."

While a sigh of relief whispered through the courtroom from those supporting pro-choice, there were many others, including other members of the high court, who were not pleased at all. Blackmum's troubles had only just begun. Although Blackmum's opinion reflected the court's majority, those disagreeing with the opinion did so with scathing, public dissents. Half of the American public was ecstatic with the ruling, the other half, furious. Blackmum, and the majority rule, had "ignited a firestorm of controversy that still rages a decade and a half later." [11] Justice Blackmum was often at the center of that controversy.

The Supreme Court has received more mail on the abortion decision than on any other case handed down. Blackmum has been called every vicious name writers could bring forth, from Hitler to Pontius Pilate. For years he has been booed when speaking publicly. His presentations and home have been picketed by anti-abortionists. Threats have been made against his life.

Yet, in 1987, in a public television interview, Blackmum quietly stated that he still stood behind the abortion decision and, in fact, considered it essential to protect women's equality.

Justice Harry Blackmum's life changed dramatically with the decision, as did the lives of millions of American women and men. An entire nation's thinking about privacy, women and personal rights were challenged with the case. Although the abortion debate still rages, Harry Blackmum was a great pioneer in opening the door to greater freedom and personal responsibility for Americans. No matter what side of the abortion issue you may adhere to, it is valuable to recognize the struggle and courage it takes to challenge *any* paradigm. Blackmum shifted a major paradigm in thinking, and his courage and vision are to be admired.

BUSINESS

W. Edwards Deming

In the late 1970's the Ford Motor company was in very serious trouble. The problem: For too long the company had been run primarily by management looking only at bottom line numbers. Attention to consumers, long range planning, and quality management had been almost completely forgotten — until W. Edwards Deming appeared on the scene.

In 1981 the president of Ford, Donald E. Petersen, called Deming and pleaded for assistance. Deming, an American statistician, had become almost a household name in Japan where he had revolutionized Japanese business. With his first meeting with Ford CEO's he began to change American business as well.

Deming's philosophy basically stated that quality management is rooted in an understanding of the power and persuasiveness of variation and how it affects the process, the delicate interaction of people, machines, materials and the environment.[12] Deming believed that quality is defined by the desires and needs of customers.

By observing Ford's operations and by carefully instructing Ford management to change from short term, bottom line managing to long term, consumer-oriented management, Deming was able to turn the Ford Motor Company around and to help it return to viable financial life.

He managed to do this amazing process in relatively short time. Soon he became highly sought after by other large American companies. Corporate America's paradigm began to shift.

Despite his ability to turn failing American corporations into thriving industry giants, Deming was not liked by all who knew him. While hourly workers loved his philosophy and sat quietly awed during his speeches, many CEO's were angered by his attacks on management and its many arrogant and sweeping mistakes of the past. Suggesting that Americans could prosper by using Japanese business techniques offended a great number of high ranking business officers. Public debate with Deming was not at all uncommon.

Although his philosophy and methods are not embraced by everyone, and while debate rages about the appropriateness of his methods, Deming was a pioneer in business. He took risks and went against the business grain. Consumers of the products of American industry can be most thankful for the outspoken courage of this man who worked to shift the thinking of American business.

EDUCATION

Christa McAuliffe

On a cold, clear day in the spring of 1986 NASA

launched the space shuttle, Challenger, and a new concept called "The Teacher-In-Space Program." Representing educators world wide, Christa McAuliffe, teacher, wife and mother of two small children, waved to cheering crowds and stepped inside the shuttle. While an excited world watched the historic event, the shuttle roared skyward. Only moments into its journey the shuttle exploded, killing all seven of the astronauts onboard. The first educator in space was silenced before she had an opportunity to teach from the edge of the universe.

Sorrow, anger, confusion and shock rippled through the United States and the entire world. How could this happen? Investigations were conducted, court battles began and the media covered each memorial service and Senate debate on the topic for months following. But as media attention turned elsewhere, healing began. Healing not only in the hearts of Christa's immediate family but in the hearts of students and educators around the globe.

In a moving speech at the National Education Association's annual convention, Christa's husband, Steve, described the gift that Christa had shared with the world. It wasn't so much that she took the risk to travel in space to teach, but more that she believed in education and that to strengthen education meant not just dreams and ideals, it meant taking action, both political and pragmatic action. Christa wanted to draw attention to the strengths and needs of education and she worked hard to make her beliefs visible.[13] She believed in the value of education and she took risks to share her beliefs with the world.

Today, we celebrate the determined courage of each person who travels into unknown territory to promote and uphold their beliefs and dreams. Christa McAuliffe was a courageous and gentle pioneer and an inspiration to educators everywhere.

SCIENCE

Nicolaus Copernicus

Nicolaus Copernicus was a very special pioneer. As a trained mathematician, his greatest wish was to calculate the motion of the sun, moon and planets in a simple, easy-to-understand and reliable manner. He began with a study of the esteemed authority on the subject, the books of the Almagest compiled by Ptolemy (70-147 A.D.). However, despite the complete acceptance of Ptolemy's theories by scientists of the day, and perhaps more importantly, the Christian church, Copernicus could not succeed with his calculations using this source. The Almagest assumed that the earth was at rest.

It was not until Copernicus abandoned a fundamental, prevailing paradigm of the time, that he was able to calculate the movements of the heavenly bodies and planets. By calculating that the earth revolved around the sun like the planets, and also turned daily upon its axis, he was able to approach the conception of the infinity of the universe. A new view of the world was offered, and it was supported by verifiable observation.[14]

Now, having realized a thirty-six year goal, Copernicus had a major dilemma before him. His work, if made public, would send the learned scientists of the day into an uproar, it would confuse the masses and it was sure to anger the church. Fearing the reactions of these entities, Copernicus held back on his knowledge and it was only on his last day of life that he held a slightly revised version of his theory in book form. He did not feel, in that lifetime, the shift caused by his theory.

Giordano Bruno

It was Giordano Bruno, a one time Dominican monk, who upon leaving the monastery began to publicly praise the work of Copernicus as a discovery that would lead the world into a new era of thought and investigation. Although he did not make the discovery, his greatest contribution was that he understood the importance of that discovery and he shared his understanding with the people. He stated,

> *"There is only one heaven, an immesurable domain of light-giving and illuminated bodies'; the Godhead is not to be sought far away from us, since we have it near to us, yes in us, more than we ourselves are in us; so must the inhabitants of other worlds not seek it in ours, since they have it in their own and in themselves."[15]*

Because of his knowledge, his understanding and his willingness to share this revolutionary information with the world, the Pope sent him to be burned at the stake. In 1600 Bruno was burned to death at the main piazza in Rome. But he had let truth and knowledge into public light and the world has never "turned" quite the same since.

CIVIL RIGHTS AND PUBLIC POLICY

Rosa Parks

Born into a poor family in Alabama in 1913, Rosa Parks grew up working very hard. As a young child she did much of the caretaking of the family as her mother, separated from Rosa's father, worked long hours away from the home. As Rosa grew and married, she took on many jobs to help support her own family. It was during her employment that she became extremely aware of the prejudice and injustices directed toward black Americans. She and her husband, Raymond Parks, became active in their community to try and reduce some of the degradation of blacks. However, it was not until December 1, 1955, that her stand for equality rocked a nation.

Sitting in the all black section in the back of an Alabama bus, Rosa refused to move and give up her seat to a white man when the all white section filled. "My feet weren't tired," she later recalled, "I'd just had enough."[16] Rosa was roughly escorted off the bus and immediately arrested. Both she and her husband lost their jobs and had to flee north to avoid dangerous harassment as the incident sparked not only city wide protests, but a year long bus boycott. One year later, the Supreme Court ruled that the segregation of public busses was unconstitutional.

By sticking to her position, no matter what the personal repercussion, Rosa Parks changed the public policy of an entire nation. With Rosa Parks, a paradigm based on fear, misunderstanding and prejudice began to shift.

There is more work to be done in the shifting of our thinking toward each other as humans. At 82, Rosa Parks continues to work to eradicate unfair treatment of people of all races. Her focus is with the education and empowerment of young people. She is indeed, a pioneer and a shifter!

YOU!

All of these people, and many, many others, make contributions to our lives by moving beyond existing, and usually limiting, beliefs. As you expand into new ways of being, you will make an impact on the lives of others and your life as well. You are a pioneer!

Let's start at the very beginning!
A very good place to start!

Teleportation!

Chapter Five

HOW DO YOU TELEPORT?

*Act as if that which you perceive in your mind
were already here in the physical world.*
Dr. Wayne Dyer,
Real Magic

*If you wish to change your relationship with matter,
understand that the more conscious you are
the less dense matter becomes.*
Gary Bonnell,
Ascension

This is probably the most important chapter you will read in this book, but that doesn't mean it's the most difficult one. Learning to teleport does not take hard work — but it does take commitment. As you read through the list of preparatory steps below, you will see that you *already know* how to do each one of these activities! The only things that have been missing in your development are the commitment to follow these steps in a routine fashion *and* the recognition that these are the steps leading to teleportation.

The following preparatory steps were developed in an evolutionary manner, as the result of a movement — no pun intended — into the world of teleportation from a class Gwen was teaching. The class was created to study a book channeled by Jane Roberts, entitled, *The Afterdeath Journal of an American Philosopher: The World View of William James.* It was during this class, one evening, that we began questioning which activities were, or were not, possible while in a physical body. This discussion led us down the road... to new classes exploring the elements of the art of dematerializing and materializing and then, to teleportation.

STEPS TO BECOMING "STEP-LESS": THE ROAD TO TELEPORTATION

1. Reading, Mental Preparation, Bending the Paradigm

Any book that discusses energy movement and expansion is of value in your preparation, even if the material does not specifically mention teleportation. If you have picked up this book, it's likely you already have some other books in your possession that explore the movement of energy. Use the written material to help open those parts of your mind that have the know-how for this way of living. These written works will act as a catalyst for your growth simply by reading them. In addition, we suggest three books as resources that may, very well, facilitate your development.

As described above, the essence of William James, through the medium Jane Roberts, awakened us with enticing, inspirational whispers of wisdom that pointed us in the direction of teleportation. Therefore, we strongly recommend *The Afterdeath Journal of an American Philosopher: The World View of William James,* as a source of mental stimulation and of opening to new ways of viewing the world in which you live.

A second valuable source of material on teleportation is a five volume series entitled, *Life and Teaching of the Masters of the Far East,* by the late Baird T. Spalding. Volumes Three and Four are especially helpful for mental preparation. Mr. Spalding witnessed and experienced the art of teleportation and provides great insights into the elements of mastery over the physical body. We offered a quote from one of his volumes in Chapter Two.

A third book, *Ascension, The Original Teachings of Christ Awareness,* by Gary Bonnell, is also mentioned in Chapter Two. Although the book deals specifically with ascension, rather than teleportation, the information provided in the "living consciously" section (pages 133-160) is excellent for developing your consciousness, a necessary and fulfilling aspect of preparing for teleportation.

And, it is our intention that the book you are now reading will inspire you to begin your journey into the world of teleportation . . . a world that is infinite in possibilities, a world that has no limitation. . . a world that is as enjoyable in its process as it is in the final product!

2.   <u>Know ... and "Go"</u>

The next step in the learning experience is to understand that you *already know* how to teleport, because you already know how to move energy. And that's what teleportation is: the movement of your physical energy — just doing it with your mind, rather than with your muscles! For example, you are constantly sending your thoughts, which are energy, into the universe. Sometimes you do this consciously, such as with telepathic communication, but often times it is unconscious on your part. All that is needed here is for you to become *conscious* of moving energy. And you do that by turning your attention to it. Right now. Rather than telling the universe (or anyone who will listen) that you hope to teleport some day, turn your attention to the movement of energy, relax, and let yourself begin the process.

In his book, *Ageless Body, Timeless Mind*, Deepak Chopra describes the power of attending to an activity:

> *"As soon as you pay attention to any function, a transformation takes place. For example, if someone puts a five-pound weight in*

Aura photography can demonstrate some amazing shifts in our energy due to the activities we undertake. These are "before and after" aura photos of Ms. Marie-Helene Roussel, one of the participants on an excusion to Bimini in the Bahamas. The first photo was taken upon her arrival on Bimini, January 7, 1995. The white, pink and lavender colors indicate she has been experiencing spiritual growth and is feeling both unconditional love and a strong connection to her spirit guides.

Photograph by Gwen Totterdale

The second photo was taken four days later. In the interim, during her time on Bimini, Ms. Roussel participated in seminars on telepathy and teleportation, dived around the Atlantis Rows of Stones and swam with wild spotted dolphins. The dark blue and aqua blue colors reflect strong mental connections/development, strongly associated with Atlantis, and stepping into emotional empowerment, oftentimes the result of being with dolphins!

Photograph by Gwen Totterdale

Photograph by Keith Woodhouse

This first aura photo was taken of Gwen Totterdale shortly after she finished channeling a daylong seminar in Michigan in February, 1995. The second photo of Gwen was also taken after a group channeling she did, this time while on tour on Bimini Island in the Bahamas in January, 1995. Quite a contrast!

Although both photos were taken after seminars in which she channeled, there are two significant differences: the locations of the seminars and the seminar topics. The first photo was taken after a seminar entitled, *Friends, Lovers and Partners: Who Are Your Soulmates?* The red and yellow colors in her auric field indicate passion (usually connected with physical relationships) and a lot of intuition in business relationships. The seminar in Michigan was, in fact, about identifying soulmate relationships in personal and professional arenas.

Photograph by Tracy O'Reilly Kohlrautz

This second photo was taken after a seminar entitled, *Transmigration: The Next Step in Intergalactic Travel!* Deep blue and white colors were dominant in her auric field, indicating mental connections/development and spiritual development/expansion of one's soul. This seminar on Bimini was the third one on developing mental psychic skills (the other two being on telepathy and teleportation).

Aside from the topics, the other discernible difference is location. In particular, the *Dolphin Discovery World Tours* excursion to Bimini was focused in large part on the Rows of Stones and ancient Atlantis, which was known for its advancements in mental activities.

Just a footnote: The sweater Gwen was wearing that evening was actually green, but appears blue in the photo because of the deep blue energy in her auric field!

Photograph by Gwen Totterdale

Rabbit Island, or *Manana*, is so named because it has a form loosely resembling that of a rabbit. Off the windward coast of O'ahu, Rabbit Island is green in the winter, brown in the summer and barren except for birds that routinely perch upon it, making it a bird sanctuary. Maybe it should be called "Bird Island," but we nicknamed it "Teleportation Island."

Photograph by Gwen Totterdale

The cliffs in this photo overlook Hulopo'e Bay, off of the Hawaiian Island of Lana'i, the *Private Isle*. Romantic Hawaiian legends tell of the cliff dwellers who are believed to inhabit some of the caves carved by sweeping ocean currents. Lana'i is as beautiful as the Aloha spirit demonstrated by the residents of this community.

Photograph by Gwen Totterdale

The wild spotted dolphins of Bimini, in the Atlantic Ocean, seek the company of snorkelers, divers and swimmers. All they need is to hear the sound of a purring motor and they race toward the boat---ready to play and swim among those of us who are neither as adept in the water nor as efficient in our breathing! Swimming among the spotted dolphins, it is easy to determine their relative ages... the more spots you see, the older the dolphin!

Photograph by Gwen Totterdale

The waters surrounding Bimini alternate between royal blue and aqua colors, encouraging an irresistible urge to dive in and cool off in its pristine waters. Directly in the center of this picture is a sequence of rocks known as Three Sisters, a name which is linked to the Pleiadian star system.

The most famous stone circle in the world, Stonehenge is a powerful, masculine, haunting remnant of ancient times. We have two views of Stonehenge here: one through the eyes of the aura camera; the other through the eyes of the visitor. The blue colors indicate a deep, universal wisdom rising from the combination of the stones themselves and their specific location... an energy vortex that is the intersection of key meridians.

Photograph by Gwen Totterdale

The energy of Stonehenge is immensely appealing, as are the mysterious energies in the surrounding fields, filled in the summer months with crop circles...pictograms of all shapes, sizes and formations that first began "appearing" in the rows of wheat, barley, etc. over a decade ago. The many mysteries of this area challenge mystics and scientists alike!

Photograph by Gwen Totterdale

In the southern, central region of England lies Glastonbury, Ancient Isle of Avalon. Glastonbury Tor, with the remains of a 12th century church rising out of it, is visible for miles, appearing as a beckoning post for those interested in exploring the realms and mysteries of Merlin, King Arthur, Guinevere and Lancelot.

Photograph by Gwen Totterdale

These photos of Jessica Severn were taken at the beginning and end of a three day weekend during which she practiced teleportation and transmigration. In the first photo, there is an incredible amount of dark blue, reflecting all of her past development in teleportation as well as her current focus of expanding her skills during the weekend.

The second photo shows a similar pattern, but with more white forming around her head, intermixed with some aqua. The white color is indicative of spiritual development/expansion of one's soul.

While it is inappropriate to make sweeping generalizations from these photos---because there are many factors that will affect an individual's auric field---it is nevertheless an interesting result worth noting!

Just a footnote: The green color in this photo is not significant to Jessica's current situation, for the area of the aura that indicates what is happening for the individual at the present time is primarily *above and below* the head, as well as what is immediately surrounding it. The colors far off to the right and left of the individual in an aura photo indicate what is being generated externally and internally and will be coming into the "picture" in a few months.

Photograph by Gwen Totterdale

*your hand and lifts it up and down for you a
hundred times, your arm won't gain any muscle
strength. However, if you perform the same action voluntarily, completely different signals are
sent from the motor cortex in your brain. Not
just your biceps but your heart and lung tis-
sues will receive increased stimulus, as will specific areas of your brain that control motor co-
ordination."* [17]

What Dr. Chopra is describing here is the difference
between active and passive learning. When you *attend* to
something, you engage in active learning.

Maybe you haven't actually taken a trip yet — a mi-
nor detail! You are a budding teleporter. You are now focusing your attention, *and intention*, on it. Don't think of teleportation as something you will learn in the future. Consider it part of your present moment knowing, become conscious of it by beginning the steps right now. Wayne Dyer
emphasized in his book, *Real Magic*, the importance of focusing and closing your mind to all distractions. He goes on
to state what we consider a universal truth:

"Focusing is your natural knowing within." [18]

3.   Use of the Herb Seawrack

Seawrack, or bladder wrack, is a useful herbal supple-
ment that is helpful in preparing the physical body for

teleportation. Also known by the names sea oak and kelpware, seawrack is a seaweed extract that is often recommended to combat obesity in individuals. Exactly how this herb facilitates the teleportation process is not known, but the results suggest that it does promote such activity. As with any herb you are considering, it is important and necessary for you to check with your herbalist, iridologist or other health practitioner to be sure that your body responds favorably to the herb. We have found that three or four drops of liquid seawrack daily, under the tongue, will be a sufficient amount for you to prepare for your teleportation experiences.

4.   Resting, Fatigue Reversal, Enlightenment through Energy

Even before starting the first classes in teleportation, Gwen kept encouraging everyone to rest. A rested body is more alert and more cooperative than a tired body. Most of the participants didn't listen. This is not surprising, given that much of our society in general does not listen — until there is a breakdown, such as an illness or disease. But remember how much easier it was to retain information in school when you were rested? How much more easily tasks could be performed after a good night's rest? The same is true here!

To rest involves making a commitment to listen to

your body and respond to its needs when it is tired, rather than pushing it to the brink of exhaustion. To rest means taking time to nurture the body in a loving way, giving yourself time to just be, without scurrying to constantly meet deadlines. To rest is to prioritize sleep, just as we prioritize some of life's other treasures, such as love, prosperity, health and joy. Giving your body rest, *real rest,* is a very important step in the teleportation process. We cannot emphasize this point enough! Please make time for rest.

5.   Meditation, Mental Rest, Mental Alertness is the Key

As you are preparing for teleportation — reading, resting, etc. — you will find it helpful to begin a schedule of meditation, setting aside the same time each day, if possible, for silence or meditation. Simply remove yourself from the noise and hassles of everyday life. Become clear by allowing your thoughts to flow through you, rather than by trying to rid yourself of unwanted thoughts. In this way you release tension by allowing a flow of energy, rather than feeling stress by actively trying to direct your thoughts. In this way you can move into deeper states of mental relaxation and begin to tap into the universal intelligence known as the unconscious.

If you have never meditated, or feel that you have never done it successfully, there are many excellent audio tapes and books available to teach you the basics. What we emphasize here is that by preparing your mind, through enhancing your state of awareness, you will begin to bring to the surface all that you need to remember in order to rapidly develop your teleportation skills.

6.   Create a Teleportation Schedule

To become proficient with teleportation, you need to practice. Creating a teleportation schedule will help you to *make time* for this practice. The desire to teleport will increase as you begin to experience success in traveling! And creating a set time for this activity, normally two to three times a week, will help you along your way.

We always encourage students to get together to teleport whenever possible. This is because of the synergy created by two or more people coming together for a common purpose. You are probably already familiar with this concept:

The whole is greater than the sum of its parts.

This is true for many metaphysical or spiritual activities performed in a group setting, such as group prayer circles, meditations, chanting, Sufi dancing and so forth. Thus, we encourage you to practice with a group, as well as on your own.

The evening hours are usually most conducive for teleportation experiences for several reasons. First, normally your evening hours are more flexible for you, and thus you are not trying to teleport while thinking about your business or family obligations during the day. Second, the energy levels in your part of the world are normally "winding down," and so there is not as much "static" in the atmosphere which can impede the teleportation process.

Third, we normally try to teleport to more secluded locations because the act of teleportation cannot interfere with prevailing cultural beliefs, in terms of "materializing" in front of someone who is not prepared to deal with the consequences of seeing what appears to defy the laws of physics. Therefore, nighttime offers us an opportunity to teleport to places where we cannot easily be seen. And fourth, to teleport at night is a more natural state for the body because, as we will discuss in Chapter Six, your body has probably experienced spontaneous teleportation while in sleep state. Traveling through the night skies takes on a mystical feeling, one you will no doubt grow to enjoy!

However, if your life is scheduled more heavily in the evening, morning may be the only time available to you. If so, the earlier the better, for all of the reasons mentioned above!

7. **State Your Intentions**

An important step, once you are ready to begin, is to

state, calmly and clearly, your intentions. Not your desires — your *intentions*. For example, you may say:

"I intend to teleport to Sunset Beach in Hawaii."

or

*"I intend to see my friend Jessica
at Stonehenge this evening."*

Wording it this way is preferable to stating what you would like to do, or try to do. Why? Because stating an intention is setting the stage for doing something, not hoping to do something. Stating your intention as an absolute, rather than a desire, is a statement to the universe that you are now ready to proceed. No fence sitting for you! The universal energies, then, will come forward to assist you, because you have become clear about your goals.

8.   <u>See Yourself in the Location You Have Chosen</u>

Of course, this is a kind of pretending — at least at first. That's okay! As the quote by Wayne Dyer at the beginning of this chapter suggests, begin by acting as if you are already where you want to be! Simply see yourself in the place where you intend to go. See yourself not as you would in dreams, as if you were watching yourself on a movie screen; rather, see your location, and you in the location, as if you were viewing it from inside your body. For example, Jessica begins by looking toward her feet, with eyes closed, and "sees" that aspect of herself in the intended location. Gwen uses mental imagery to see her body in its perfect state, and in the perfect location, where she wants to be. Some people report that they begin by focusing on their hands, solar plexus, or even their toes. Whatever you choose to do, be sure to see, and *feel*, yourself in the place where you intend to be!

9.   Allow Yourself to Feel the Energy in Your Body ... Breathe!

You will notice that your body feels as if it is spiraling upward. Your energy twirls around, upwardly moving, like the stripes on a candy cane or barber's pole. Although others near you will not see it, you will feel your energy swirling within you, leading you to sway a bit, possibly, or to feel lightheaded. It is very important to remember to breathe — consciously — during this process. As these physical sensations appear there is a tendency to hold your breath, so become conscious of your breathing pattern. Take slow, smooth, deep breaths. Remember that teleportation is a mental activity, and so you need active brain cells to help you accomplish your goal. And brain cells need oxygen — lots of it!

Teleportation!

There is a nine point teleportation process we offer in our seminars. If you can consciously focus on these concepts, your body will take care of the rest.

The concepts to keep in mind are, in order:

1. *Lift your eyes skyward*

2. *Give yourself permission to FLY!*

3. *Acknowledge your right of sovereignty*

4. *Trust in who you are*

5. *The power to create is a power to emanate (to flow out, issue, proceed)*

6. *To get there, LOVE what you know is there*

7. *Recognize that life is only a lesson when we want it to be*

8. *Feel the magic of movement*

9. *Realize your dream*

Some people report feeling slightly nauseous during the initial stages of teleportation. If you experience this, don't worry. It will pass very quickly. Others report a sexual sensation in their bodies, similar to the feelings of moving toward orgasm. If you experience *this*, on the other hand, you probably don't want it to pass too quickly! Jessica experiences a feeling of tightness across the area of her third eye, as if there were a tight band around her head. Whatever sensations you experience, they will lead into the next sensation...

10.   A "POP"

This is not so much an effortful step as it is an automatic one. Instantly, and probably briefly, you will find yourself in another location! One way to describe this experience is to liken it to SCUBA divers who begin to ascend toward the surface from the depths of the water. As a diver begins to move upward, closer to the surface, her inflated vest creates a tendency to accelerate movement until "POP," the diver breaks the surface, and pops into a different reality, above water!

When you first begin to experience teleportation, it is not uncommon to feel that you are seeing your location as if through a keyhole. Looking at a site this way means you can only see a small portion of the scene. Your view will expand as you practice. Also, it may feel as if your *entire body* did not make the trip, that only segments of your body teleported. Another very common experience is to feel as if you are there only for a moment or two. Again, the more you practice, the more complete your experience will become.

And you will see not only the entire location, but you will feel and smell it as well — sand beneath your feet, warm sea breezes, dry and dusty back-roads, etc.

11.   <u>Finding Your Way Home</u>

Coming home from your teleportation trip is easy. In fact, initially you probably won't have much say in the matter! For a split second you are standing beneath the towering giants of Stonehenge ... the next moment you are sitting in an easy chair in your living room. You give it another try. With a "POP" you find yourself at the edge of a clear, still lake. Then a quick retreat to that easy chair again! And you are exhausted. Although the total teleportation time is very brief, you are so tired you must drag your body to bed.

What happened? Congratulations! You did it!! Teleportation exercises your mental muscles — parts of the brain you have probably not been using, at least for that purpose. Teleportation, as noted earlier, takes a lot of brain power! Consider exhaustion a sign of success. With time, the exhaustion will give way to exhilaration! So go to bed...you earned it!

Now you know how to travel!
Ready to go? Timing is everything.....

Chapter Six

WHEN DOES TELEPORTATION OCCUR?

But in the next instant
she began to feel the sensation of energy ...
This was followed by a "pop" felt in the top of her head.

Gwen's spontaneous teleportation

Sherri had been in the middle of a bad dream,...
a friend of hers appeared in her bedroom and held her hand.
Sherri's friend told her everything was okay
and that she was just having a nightmare.

Sherri W's view of a teleportation, Seattle, WA.

In our continuing research into the many aspects of teleportation, we discovered early on that sometimes the experience of teleportation "happens upon us," rather than being a conscious effort on our part to create this event. One of Gwen's earliest teleportation experiences occurred in her shower. Gwen was at home one Saturday morning, taking a shower, with eyes closed, shampooing her hair. A fairly routine experience we've all had, with the steady stream of warm water splashing against her. In the next instant she began to feel the sensation of energy swirling upward in her body, a "spinning" of sorts. This was followed by a "pop" felt in the top of her head. She immediately felt panicky and, without understanding why, kept her eyes tightly closed. She had an inner knowing that her external reality had somehow changed.

And it had! When she finally dared to open her eyes, she found herself in a shower stall that was the polar opposite of the one in her home: sliding glass doors were where the wall was supposed to be and vice versa; the shower head and she, herself, were faced in the opposite direction. She blinked hard, and opened her eyes again, but the scene remained unchanged. Closing her eyes a second time, heart racing, she felt another involuntary "pop" that was less intense than the first one, and knew instinctively she was back in her shower, her reality. She opened her eyes to find everything back to the way it originally was.

What happened? This experience is what we refer to as a spontaneous teleportation. The event was neither planned nor directed by Gwen, at least not consciously. In fact, this event occurred before she began teaching teleportation classes! Nevertheless, in this experience her external reality had shifted and she found herself, for a few moments, in a new location, without benefit of physical movement. This, by definition, is teleportation.

Teleportation, we have found, can actually occur in any of the following three ways:

1. *Spontaneous teleportation*
2. *Directed teleportation in sleep state*
3. *Directed conscious teleportation*

We will examine each of these in turn.

SPONTANEOUS TELEPORTATION

As discussed above, spontaneous teleportation occurs to you, rather than you setting out to teleport. Have you ever had the experience of walking along a road or beach, when suddenly you are much further "down the road" or you've reached your destination but do not remember getting there? Or that it took much less time than it normally would? Perhaps you have had the experience of washing the dishes or performing some other routine activity when, for just a moment, you seem to have been somewhere else, literally to some other location.

It is likely you have experienced a spontaneous teleportation, without realizing what happened — just a feeling that something very unusual took place. One example of this kind of experience was described by a student named Kristi who was driving round-trip from San Diego to Los Angeles. Driving to L.A. took two and one half hours — a typical time in slow traffic. However, her return trip was timed at one hour and forty minutes, even though the traffic patterns were no different than before. She had the distinct feeling, during the return trip, of jumping from one spot to the next, losing gaps of the freeway as she traveled.

Gwen related Kristi's experience to a story about ancient Atlantis — an area known for utilizing teleportation — where boat travelers experienced "skipping across waters" to get to their destinations more quickly during times of rough seas or time urgency. It appears that Kristi's experience paralleled that of the ancient Atlanteans!

Spontaneous teleportation can, by definition, occur at any time — even during sleep state. One morning, at work, Jessica's secretary, Sherri, described what she called, "the most incredible dream of my entire life!" Sherri had been in the middle of a bad dream, a nightmare, when a girlfriend appeared in her bedroom and held her hand. Sherri's friend told her everything was okay and that she was just having a nightmare. Then her friend told Sherri to wake up. She did, to a room that was quiet, peaceful and empty.

Later that morning Sherri received a telephone call from that same friend, who said, "You had a bad dream, didn't you?" Before she could reply beyond a simple yes, the friend continued, "You had a bad dream and I came and held your hand and told you it was okay. Then I told you to wake up."

What Sherri referred to as an incredible dream was, in all likelihood, a spontaneous teleportation on the part of her friend. The fact that she saw her friend in her bedroom indicates it was a teleportation, not astral travel. The fact that Sherri's friend remembered the experience is even more telling.

This experience speaks for itself, in terms of its impact on the awareness of these two friends about what the human species is capable of doing. The deeper questions of why her friend was compelled to come to Sherri at that time and the importance of remembering the experience are yet to be explored. But it seems that we are capable of "traveling," even when the body is in a less active state!

You may or may not remember a spontaneous teleportation, especially if it occurs during the night. Again, a rested body will increase your chances of remembering these experiences. You may be wondering what is the point of having a teleportation experience if you cannot remember it! The importance, here, is that it indicates that your inner intelligence already *knows* how to do this! And so, with practice, you can begin to tap into this resource on a conscious level.

Although you can spontaneously teleport in sleep state, it is also possible to *direct* yourself to teleport during this time period as well, as we will discuss next.

DIRECTED TELEPORTATION IN SLEEP STATE

This second type of teleportation experience also occurs in sleep state, but it is consciously directed by you. Before going to sleep, simply and clearly state your intention to have a teleportation experience that night. Stating your intention, with a focus on teleportation, will let the universe support your request after you go to sleep. You may want to specify a particular location, or you can simply request to teleport at some time during the night.

Remember that this experience is quite different from dreaming, because in teleportation you literally relocate your body from one point to another. How will you know the difference? When dreaming, you are normally confronted with symbols. These symbols are not necessarily real, but rather represent elements of your unconscious mind. During dreaming, there is usually a message that you are being given. In teleportation, on the other hand, you are actively relocating to another place, gathering knowledge about the place or the people you're visiting.

If it is a dream, when you awaken you will carry the feeling tone of the dream; sometimes the dream is hazy, even confusing. A teleportation experience, on the other hand, feels like a memory, or event, and is usually more pointed and clear, with the remembrance of a physical sensation.

In July of 1993, Gwen was visiting Glastonbury, a community in southern England that is the center of activity concerning England's famous crop circles. Glastonbury, from the days of King Arthur and Lancelot, has been referred to as the Ancient Isle of Avalon. Gwen was staying in a bed and breakfast with a view of majestic Glastonbury Tor from her room. The Tor is one of the places we have identified as a place conducive to teleportation experiences (see Chapter Seven). Her room had an opening onto a private patio via a beautiful glass French door, bordered on either side by floor to ceiling windows. It was from here that she could see the Tor. One night, while preparing for bed, Gwen asked for a teleportation experience to the Tor. She stated her intention to go there during sleep state, closed the door to the patio, pulled heavy velvet drapes across the windows and door, and crawled into bed.

Upon awaking the next morning, Gwen had an immediate remembrance of "traveling" to the Tor, and felt tired even though she had been asleep for eight hours. But she remembered something else, something significant: the feel of the velvet drapes in her hands. Waking with the sensation in her hands, she realized the feeling came not from the previous evening, but from the middle of the night. She looked over to find that the drapes were pulled all the way back, exposing the windows, door, and light from outside. It was as if, upon returning from the Tor, she stopped to pull the drapes apart before "popping" back into bed. But why?

Sometimes we do things during sleep state to spark a remembrance later. Moving the drapes in that room at night would have been very difficult, because a heavy wooden chair was situated between her bed and the French door: getting to the drapes in the dark would have been close to impossible. But if teleportation had occurred, then there was no physical movement, just physical relocation! Therefore, one can travel with ease from location to location, without bumping into things in the middle of the night!

Gwen's remembrance of "feeling the texture of the drapes" is, as we mentioned earlier, not uncommon as teleportation skills expand. As you continue to focus your attention on teleportation, even in sleep state, you will have more and more of these experiences.

But why wait until you go to sleep? The following describes the kind of teleportation you were preparing for in Chapter Five!

DIRECTED CONSCIOUS TELEPORTATION

This type of teleportation is planned. Set aside a time and place where you will be undisturbed and comfortable and where you can consciously focus your energies. As we discussed in the previous chapter, it is usually best to teleport later in the evening or in the early morning hours.

When you first begin teleporting consciously, your sense of direction may not be the best. Over and over, with ourselves and others, we have relayed experiences where we intend to bring in one location and actually end up somewhere else! Call it the "Wrong Way Corrigan" syndrome, or whatever, but sometimes we intend to teleport to Bimini and end up in another part of the world — literally. One of Jessica's earlier experiences in Seattle, Washington is just such an example. As she describes it:

When Does Teleportation Occur?

A couple of years ago I had quite a surprise while teleporting. I intended to meet with Gwen and Elizabeth (a fellow teleporter) at a specific location. Something happened and I ended up on the inside of the closed market isles of the Pike Place market, a waterfront shopping area in downtown Seattle. I saw metal roll-down doors used to secure the market at night and realized where I had landed. Suddenly I saw another person looking at me. I couldn't tell if it was a young man or woman. It was clear the other person saw me as well. We were both startled by each other's presence. Cautiously we began to speak.

"You're not supposed to be able to see me."

"Not unless we're both teleporting!"

We were awed! Looking around we saw a pile of crushed ice on the floor, close to one of the fish stands:

"What do you see?"

"Ice. And you?"

"Ice."

We got very excited when we both identified a lighted exit sign. In the next second I was gone from the market and back in my bedroom at home. But I know I met another teleporter out there!

Just for the record, neither Gwen nor Elizabeth saw Jessica at their predestined meeting that evening... she never left Seattle! But her experience was one for the books ... and for *our* book!

Teleportation!

In another experience of directed teleportation, Gwen set her sights on a preferred location called Rabbit Island in Hawaii (see Chapter Seven). However, she "overshot" her destination and popped onto a beach five miles south of there in Hawaii Kai. Don't worry about getting lost. It happens to most teleporters in the beginning. As you practice, your skills will sharpen and you will arrive in the desired place. Relax, too, in the knowledge that when you are first learning, you will automatically "pop" back to your place of departure.

Sometimes you will make more than one stop in your teleportation travels. Gwen will sometimes experience "making a few visits" during a teleportation trip back to Hawaii when she is away from home. This is also a function of *how long* you are able to teleport. You may go for only a few seconds or for several minutes.

Your directed conscious teleportation experiences will magnify over time. It has been our experience that teleportation skills develop in a nonlinear fashion. In other words, you may have several practice sessions with a glimpse or two of success, and then in the next session you may have a major breakthrough! As you experience these successes, you will look forward to further expansion and new destinations!

When the student is ready, the teacher will appear.
When the teleporter is ready,
the location will appear!
Let's go!

Chapter Seven

WHERE CAN YOU GO?

To fly as fast as thought,
to anywhere that is,
you must begin by knowing
that you have already arrived.
Richard Bach,
Jonathan Livingston Seagull

All the world's a stage,
and all the men and women
merely players.
William Shakespeare,
As You Like It

The possibilities associated with teleportation can bring to mind images of traveling to exotic locations, visiting friends far away, or exciting discoveries waiting to happen. However, first things first! Just as when you were first learning to ride a bicycle you wouldn't plan a cross country bicycle trip, it is normally a good idea to stay *closer to home* as you are developing your teleportation techniques.

85

We recommend you begin your process and practice by specifying familiar, local spots as your desired destinations. For example, in our first class in teleportation, held in Gwen's living room, Gwen suggested a nearby destination — her bedroom. Most of the participants had not seen that part of her home, so it was a good opportunity on two counts: (1) it was "close by" and (2) the group members could later check to see if they could correctly identify some of the items in that location.

The results were very encouraging. Although most participants could not see the entire room, they were able to identify bits and pieces of what they saw — they described their experiences as similar to "looking through an old-fashioned keyhole." One person saw a portion of the clock radio; another observed a "tiny face," later identified as a broach lying on the dresser. A shaggy rug lying atop the carpeting was sighted by another participant; and one noticed part of the intercom system hanging on the wall. Also of note: all participants agreed they were only able to remain in the bedroom for a split second. Isn't this similar to staying up on the bicycle for only a few moments your first time out?

As you develop further in teleportation, you will find that it is easier, and almost automatic, to go to different places. The distance to any particular place has no bearing on your success once you become an experienced teleporter.

There are some locations that are very conducive to the experience of teleportation:

*Some places seem to link up with other
places, like meridians of energy on the body.
Ayers Rock, Mt. Rainier, Glastonbury Tor share
a line of flow... Many of us are guided to visit
first one site, then another. As they arrange
themselves in our minds, we become the trans-
mitters which create and reinforce the links of
the chains.[19]*

Through her research into energy vortices, Gwen has
identified several areas where it is easier to cross the thresh-
old for purposes of teleportation. These "hot spots" are significant in that they draw largely on the use of mental energies, which is consistent with the development of teleportation skills.

THE ISLAND OF LANA'I, *Hawaii*

Lana'i is a small, sparsely populated island in the
middle of the Hawaiian Island chain. Located near the well-
known island of Maui, Lana'i is the only place in Hawaii
where, from the highest elevation point of Lana'i Hale, at
3,370 feet, you can see as many as five other islands — O'ahu,
Maui, Moloka'i, Kaho' olawe and the Big Island of Hawai'i.
Lana'i has a soft, gentle energy which reflects the spirit of
this small community of 2,200 residents. The energy is almost inspirational, with a magical quality that speaks to
you in the peacefulness of the early morning hours or the
windy sounds of the night skies.

Several areas on the island feel especially powerful, and one in particular, the Garden of the Gods, feels almost *other-worldly*. Lana'i is picturesque with its dramatic red-ridged cliffs rising out of the deep, blue ocean waters. So any place on this island is thrilling to see! When you teleport to Lana'i you will find it is an easy transition that can help you get away from the noise and business of everyday living.

STONEHENGE, *England*

One of the great mysteries of our planet, Stonehenge represents the furthermost reaches of imagination and possibilities known to humankind. Situated in the countryside of south central England, this famous stone circle is visited by thousands of tourists everyday. Regardless of background, culture or beliefs, visitors who arrive at Stonehenge experience feelings that are indefinable and which, for some, border on mystical.

The most common question about Stonehenge concerns how the bluestones, some with weights over forty tons, could have been transported from their native region of southern Wales. But perhaps the more intriguing question is: Why would they choose that site, the location where Stonehenge was built? There is, in fact, a strong energy vortex in and around that area that is conducive for personal growth, psychic development and advanced states of awareness. An ideal setting for teleportation! This is the likely reason for the creation there of a stone circle, especially one that is in direct alignment with the sun on the day of the summer solstice, June 21st! Throughout the year, the shadows cast upon the stones as the sun rises and sets mark the passage of the seasons, somewhat like a three-dimensional calendar.

Stonehenge, then, is a remarkable spot to visit, via automobile or teleportation. We highly recommend teleportation — not only is it less expensive, but by going there at night, you will not have to contend with the crowds! Also, although a change in its accessibility is under discussion, Stonehenge is currently "roped off" so that visitors cannot actually touch the stones. An inconvenience easily overcome since, with practice, teleportation allows you to land anywhere you please! An equally impressive stone circle at Avebury is close by and would also be an energizing place to visit.

THE ISLAND OF BIMINI, *The Bahamas*

On the western edge of the Bahamas, only 55 miles from Miami, is a long, narrow strip of land called Bimini. Known locally as a premier spot for deep sea fishing, Bimini has also achieved fame internationally as a favorite spot for the late Ernest Hemingway (known as the favored son at the Complete Angler pub), the not-so-secret hideaway for former presidential candidate Gary Hart and the location of the final scene in the Academy Award winning film, *Silence of the Lambs.* But Bimini is known for another reason: in 1940 Edgar Cayce, often referred to as the sleeping prophet, predicted while in trance state that in 1968 or 1969 the western edge of the lost continent of Atlantis would be discovered in shallow waters off of the land of Bimini.

In 1968, Dr. J.M. Valentine discovered what is now referred to as *The Great Bimini Road,* a long "reversed J-shaped" row of stones in approximately fifteen feet of water, off the northwest side of Bimini. The stones, which are actually limestone blocks, are not indigenous to that area. All attempts to remove the stones from the ocean for further examination have failed. In fact, the overriding feeling after many mishaps — cables breaking, rocks splitting in half — was to leave the row of stones *intact*, without any external interference.

Gwen has conducted numerous seminars on teleportation during her **Dolphin Discovery World Tours** excursions in that part of the world. (See photo inserts.) The energies in that area are extremely conducive to the experience of teleportation, which is no surprise when you consider that some Atlanteans, those who were very advanced mentally, routinely used both telepathy and teleportation skills in their day to day activities. A June 17, 1990 article on Bimini in *The Miami Herald* reports:

> *The search for Atlantis, the ancient,*
> *fabled land of ivory-roofed golden palaces, ideal*

*government and maybe even flying machines,
has gone on since 300 B.C. when the Greek philosopher Plato wrote of it in his works **Critias**
and **Timarus**.*

*But (in the 1900's) Edgar Cayce, a sev-
enth-grade dropout, stationery salesman, Sunday school teacher and much-heralded "sleeping prophet," went into his hypnotic trances and
made a prediction:*

*"The sunken portion of Atlantis ... a por-
tion of the temples, may yet be discovered under the slime of ages of sea water near what is
known as Bimini, off the coast of Florida. Expect it in 1968 and 1969; not so far away."*

*... David D. Zink, a former U.S. Air Force
Academy English Professor intrigued with the
origins of myths, arrived to study it in 1974...
Zink believes many civilizations, separated
widely in both history and geography, came to
understand that the earth's natural magnetic
and electrical energy flows closer to the surface
at certain places. At those sites, which girdle
the earth in a geodesic dome pattern, they built
their sacred temples.*

*It also explains the "healing hole." Hid-
den beneath mangrove thickets on nearby East
Bimini Island is a natural freshwater spring,
slightly radioactive, heavy in sulfur, which most
doctors agree is good for bursitis and arthritis. [20]*

These gravitational and electrical forces were discussed by Cayce in some of the seven hundred "Life Readings" he did that discussed the questioners' lives/connec-
tions with Atlantis. Cayce channeled that some Atlanteans

misused the power generated through their crystals leading to the destruction of Atlantis. As the article states:

> *The end began when the Atlanteans be-
> came corrupt and developed the "fire stone," a
> "terrible mighty crystal" of incredible force. It
> was to be for good, to control the "great ani-
> mals overrunning the earth." But somehow its
> rays "set in motion the fires in the inner por-
> tions of the earth," and volcanoes destroyed
> Atlantis.*

Bimini is a special, enlivening place, perfect for the
development of mental psychic abilities. We encourage you
to make Bimini a regular port-of-call during your teleportation travels!

RABBIT ISLAND, *Hawaii*

Off the windward side of O'ahu and directly across
from an oceanarium called Sea Life Park, is Rabbit Island,
a tuff cone of 60+ acres, with a maximum elevation of 200
feet. Known in the Hawaiian language as *Manana*, Rabbit
Island provides a picturesque backdrop for Sea Life Park
and the sights and sounds of dolphins leaping, sea lions bark-
ing and Hawaiian story-telling. And it is magical in its own
right, for several people have recalled teleporting to Rabbit
Island, particularly during their sleep. One of the things
sometimes remembered about their experience was *seeing*
the energy of dolphins while there. This is an intriguing

concept to explore, because some channeled information about the dolphins and ancient Atlantis suggests that dolphins also have well-developed skills for teleporting. It is possible, then, that the reason Rabbit Island is a strong teleportation site is because it is in close proximity to both the dolphins at Sea Life Park and, of course, the wild bottlenose and spinner dolphins that play in the ocean waters of windward O'ahu. Another incentive — as if you need one — to teleport to Rabbit Island!

MT. McKINLEY, *Alaska*

Mt. McKinley, known in ancient language as *Denali*, or "High One," is in the Alaskan Range of mountains, located in Denali National Park in south-central Alaska. On a clear day you can see Mt. McKinley from Anchorage, which is understandable when you realize that, at 20,320 feet, it is the highest mountain in North America. The highest point in the world is Mt. Everest, when you measure from sea level. However, if you measure from base (the bottom of the mountain) to peak, Mt. McKinley is the highest in the world, at over 18,000 feet. Quite a hike by foot! However, with teleportation not only are you able to get to the top without huffing and puffing — you can do so in record time and safely!

GLASTONBURY TOR, *England*

As one approaches the town of Glastonbury in Somerset, England, there is a very revealing sign along the roadway, informing you of the time and place you are about to enter:

Welcome to
Glastonbury
Ancient Isle of Avalon

Glastonbury is rich in metaphysical overtones, Arthurian legends and psychic energy! From Glastonbury Abbey to Chalice Well to the Tor itself, a walk through the fields of Glastonbury is like a journey back into time immortal. This energy spot is alive with the chivalry of the knights of the Round Table and the magic of Merlin, leaving you with the feeling that nothing has changed and yet nothing will ever be the same for you again! The areas in and around Glastonbury have also been linked with mappings of the twelve signs of the zodiac; many astrologers have made connections of key points on the land that, by connecting these points, reflect the heavenly formations of Scorpio, Leo, Pisces, etc.

As we mentioned in Chapter Six about the different types of teleportation, Gwen experienced a directed teleportation in sleep state in which she went to the Tor. She has also experienced other teleportation travels during her metaphysical tours in Glastonbury, including landings in other parts of England and visits to loved ones in Hawaii. Once she even "popped" into Jessica's newly built cottage in Seattle. All of this travel originated from Glastonbury, which is an indication of its power as a launch site, as well as an amazing place to visit.

The Tor, which literally means hill, is 520 feet high with a beckoning tower perched upon it, the remains of a 12th century church known as St. Michael's. The church was destroyed by a landslide in 1271. It is believed that the structure had been erected over a 5th century castle that had connections to Avalon. According to the legends of Avalon and the *Lady of the Lake*, Viviane, the only way to reach Avalon was to travel by boat across the waters. And this could only be done when the mists were raised, for Avalon was a magical place to come to only by invitation. Although marshlands surround the Tor today, centuries ago these surrounding lands were under water, lending support to the idea that the Tor was the hub of Avalon. Glastonbury Tor, with its green terraced slopes, has the look of a massive spiral — much like the flow of your energy during a teleportation experience!

TINTAGEL, *England*

Closely connected to the legends of Avalon and Camelot is the town of Tintagel, high atop the cliffs of south-western England that overlook the powerful currents of the Atlantic Ocean, which continually sculpt these cliffs. The castle ruins at Tintagel are believed to be the 5th century birthplace of King Arthur. Walking along the windswept, dramatic sites provided by its natural surroundings, one can easily envision life at Tintagel. The location for the castle was likely chosen because of its accessibility by both land and water and because it could be easily defended — in such a location a sneak attack would be virtually impossible.

In an article entitled "Walking in Albion: Chronicles of Plan-Net Geomancy" (*The Quest, Spring, 1992*), Tintagel is described as a very powerful location on our planet, following the ley lines of the earth in a geomantic flow:

> *"Tintagel is a good place to make plans and formulate wishes...Tintagel is aflame in the tints of angels, a magnificient rainbow kaleidoscope of cosmic and angelic energies. The tints of angels surround the Arthur light at domed Tintagel."*

Some of the stone structures rising from the ocean waters surrounding Tintagel bear an eerie resemblance to the cliffs of Lana'i, on the other side of the world! As the clouds roll in and over this unique community, it is possible to take a step back in time to a period of new beginnings, the birth of the future King of Camelot!

AYERS ROCK, *Australia*

In the red center of the huge continent of Australia, Ayers Rock rises up from the seemingly endless miles of desert-like conditions known as the Outback. *Uluru,* the Aboriginal name for Ayers Rock, is one of the world's largest monoliths: it is over 1,100 feet high, and is surrounded by a national park that is jointly operated by the Traditional Aboriginal Community and the Australian National Parks & Wildlife Service. Hundreds of thousands of visitors arrive each year, many longing to climb it (a challenging experience!), others content to watch the changing colors of Uluru throughout the day, especially at sunrise and sunset. From red to orange, gold, gray, brown and magenta, the combination of the sun's position and varying cloud formations gives Ayers Rock many "looks."

Known as the location of the rainbow serpent of the dreamtime, or *Tjukurpa,* the Aborigines relied on their advanced dreaming abilities as a way of receiving guidance from spirit for their daily activities and survival. They were also believed to possess advanced telepathic skills. The base of Uluru is covered with drawings and other markings made by the earlier inhabitants, showing scenes of a culture estimated to be in existence more than 40,000 years! A visit to this powerful vortex will lead you to new discoveries of ancient wisdom about nature and spirit.

Teleportation!

These are just some of the *high energy* places that exist on our planet. As you begin to venture beyond your neighborhood, we recommend all of these places for your education, expansion and enjoyment. There will be other sites you will want to visit as your teleportation skills expand. And there are many other worlds waiting to be discovered.

What lies beyond the horizon of the earth plane? Another world, of course ...

Chapter Eight

ADVANCED "TRAVEL" - TRANSMIGRATION

Angels watchin' over me oh Lord,
Angels watchin' over me.

Traditional Folk Song

It is not such a big step between your reality and mine.
There is a belief that you who are in physical form
are the only solid existence in the universe.
This is clearly not true.

Emmanuel

Transmigration is defined in *Webster's New World Dictionary* as the act of the soul passing into another body at death, as in Hindu religious beliefs. However, *transmigration* is the word Gwen was given during her research in teleportation, to describe *the passing into another dimension in order to directly communicate with spirit guides and / or teachers.* These entities likewise pass into another dimension in order to establish communication with you. The communication is face to face (so to speak), but it occurs beyond this dimension. Therefore, it is like teleportation in that your body relocates, but it is different in that you are "moving" out of this world and into another realm, what we would call a new realm of consciousness.

If you look at the two components of this word, *trans* and *migration*, it is easy to understand why Spirit selected this word to describe such an experience:

> *"Trans" is defined as a prefix*
> *meaning over, across or beyond.*

> *"Migration" is defined as*
> *a group of people settling in another*
> *country or region.*

Thus transmigration indicates a group coming together beyond their country or region of origin. And this is what the experience of transmigration feels like: a coming together of you, in physical body, and your spirit guides, for the purposes of greater understanding, knowledge and enlightenment.

The technique for transmigration is the same as that for teleportation; therefore you follow the same steps as outlined in Chapter Five. When you state your intention in step seven, however, adjust the wording to:

I intend to have a transmigration this evening.

You do not have to designate a person or location; the transmigration will be set up by your guides and teachers so you only need to state your intention of transmigrating.

If you know your guides, however, ask for them by name. If not, simply ask for a transmigration experience with the guide who, at that time, is most appropriate to assist you with the issues in your life. In that case state clearly that you seek a being who comes in light, in your best interests and with love.

It is important to focus first on developing your teleportation skills before beginning the transmigration process. However, after the teleportation steps and process become automatic, and once you are more comfortable with this technique, it would work well to set a schedule in which you practice doing a transmigration following your teleportation experience. As we indicated earlier, you may be very tired after the events of the evening. But like riding bicycles, the more you develop "your muscles" along these lines, the less fatiguing your future experiences will be.

Why would you want to experience transmigration? To answer this, it is important to first discuss the unique motivations behind both teleportation and transmigration. With teleportation, we began to experience a new way of directing our energy, consciously, and with the purpose of relocating to other destinations. As mentioned in Chapter Three, our internal need to expand beyond limitations, and to develop new, easier ways to connect with other people and locations, is the motivating factor for developing this skill.

With transmigration, on the other hand, while we are

still wanting to expand our energy and to connect with others, we purposefully intend to communicate with our spirit guides and teachers. Why? In order to better understand what is happening in our lives, what past life experiences may be currently influencing us and what light and knowledge these beings, from a broader vantage point, can impart to us. Communicating with them is like getting a psychic reading, but it is more immediate, more interactive, and more revealing in a feeling sense. You understand what your guides are communicating to you on an emotional level, not just on a spiritual or mental level.

We have all had experiences where we knew that we were being watched over or guided. If, for example, you are crossing a street and feel as if you are suddenly pulled back — only to see a car speeding by you — you might feel that this presence was an *angel on your shoulder*. Or perhaps you have been down emotionally and felt abandoned by others, then in the next instant you received a flash of emotional support or turned on the television to see the words: *You are not alone.* These are examples similar in feeling tone to a transmigration experience. The one significant difference is that you decide, in a conscious transmigration, to relocate to a meeting place with your guides.

In a transmigration experience, the communication is telepathic. In other words, you communicate mind to mind, rather than with spoken words. Also, in a transmigration time appears to stop, because you are not in *earth time* since you are relocating to a different dimension. In teleportation the clock keeps ticking, because you never travel out of this time-operated dimension. Your experience of meeting, talking and relating to your guide or guides will seem "time consuming," but when you return from the transmigration you will find that only a few moments have gone by ... just the time it takes to ready yourself for the transmigration experience.

Whatever information you are given during the transmigration, the overwhelming feeling when you are in it is one of connecting with those who love you unconditionally and without judgment. Some may experience it in a similar fashion to the ghosts of Christmas taking Scrooge to see the events of his life. Others will feel reunited with guides whom they have know from another lifetime or galaxy. And many will feel very protected, supported and embraced, similar to a feeling of "going home."

One of Jessica's profound experiences in transmigration occurred early in her process of learning to teleport. She describes it this way:

> I remember a transmigration where I met the Angel of New Beginnings. I found myself standing in a dark room — actually there were no walls, ceiling or floor but I was standing. Coming toward me was a beautiful being, a woman, with very long dark hair flowing around her. Her dress shimmered and seemed to float to one side although I felt no wind or breeze.
> I don't know how, or why, but I immediately recognized her. I felt filled with love. She

seemed to be holding out her arms toward me. Then I saw what appeared to be a giant egg carton filled with glowing "eggs." They looked like gleaming, white billiard balls to me.

"Are these babies?" I asked.

"They're souls," she replied, smiling gently.

Then the angel pointed through the clouds onto a scene. I saw myself on an island, typing on my computer. A group of children stood around me. I was smiling and happy and so were the children. My present self began to cry a bit and I asked the angel if I had "done it" — meaning the transmigration.

"Yes, my dear, of course you did. And you will get very good at it so that you can assist with their transition." She nodded toward the "eggs."

I remember thinking that I should hurry and write everything down but I felt the message not to worry, I would remember it. Then I "came out of it." I couldn't wait for Gwen to call the class back so that I could share this experience.

Several years later, when I began to write and sell children's literature, I understood what the Angel had shown me. Everything that happened during the experience makes sense to me now.

Transmigration experiences can involve brief messages or extended teachings. For example, it is common to connect with one guide who shows you experiences you've had in a past life that are affecting your life today. Other times you will meet and interact with a guide or teacher who, as with Jessica's experience above, informs you of things that are coming up in your life.

Sometimes you will be contacted in advance of your transmigration experience, usually in dream state. During the transmigration you will be reminded of a dream you had that you didn't quite understand when it occurred. Your guide will explain its meaning and implications during your transmigration experience.

Another mode your guides may use in a transmigration is one where they demonstrate how they are operating in your life, i.e. how they are assisting you. This teaching is universal, in the sense that they help you understand more about the cosmic purpose they have in your life. For example, in a recent transmigration, Gwen was shown a concept called the *Council of One*. This circular council chamber — similar to a round table, or wheel, with spokes in it, in a conference room without walls — included guides and teachers who came in and out of it, reporting on how they were assisting Gwen. Rather than focusing on the information, Gwen's guide requested that she look at the process and how it was operating. As each guide stepped into the circle, a color was illuminated underneath, which indicated the area that would be addressed — blue concerned mental development, red indicated relationships, etc. One guide was presiding over the council, and coordinated the information given. Not all "seats" were taken, just those where the guides had information to report. Gwen was also told, telepathically, that the guide giving the report did not speak in terms of problems; instead, this guide discussed what opportunities and new solutions were being implemented, and how each would benefit the current issue.

Coming out of the transmigration experience, Gwen had an immediate understanding, and feeling, of how guides operate through the power of love, not out of fear. She understood that they did not view events in a person's life as limitations. Instead, they focused on what was happening that might provide new opportunities for moving ahead and transforming situations. In other words, they look forward to the possibilities with a positive, not a negative, attitude. Having this glimpse into the *cosmos* puts another piece of the cosmic puzzle into place! We will not see the entire process, presumably, while in a physical body, but each new concept helps us understand more of the bigger picture, and thus to operate from a greater state of knowing.

Feedback from many of those developing their transmigration skills indicates they are thoroughly enjoying the process and the connection with their guides. We trust you will too!

And now, does anyone have a question?
Let's explore some more...

Chapter Nine

BUT WHAT ABOUT???

*Transferring into the Fourth Dimension
is a very graceful exiting of physical
limitations and beliefs of limitation.
It is very gently letting go.*

MARKAS

*Follow your heart
and don't be afraid.*

Anonymous

Having spent the past several years practicing and studying teleportation, we have found this to be an exciting method of travel, and so want to share it with others. As Gwen has said... "Some people like to live in Cleveland, some like to live in Hawaii. It's a big world and there's something here for all of us!" Of course, not everyone is interested in learning to teleport. Just as some people enjoy traveling by air and others prefer travel over land, this method of travel will appeal to some, but not to others. Still, we are finding that more and more people are interested, curious, perhaps even enthusiastic, about trying teleportation. And, there are many people who have had a teleportation experience but simply didn't know what was happening at the time!

No matter what the interest level, however, there is always a host of questions generated by a discussion of teleportation. Perhaps you've been asking a few questions as you've been reading this book. In the next few pages we'll answer some of the questions that have come up in our own work and some that have been generated by our students in seminars and workshops. The answers have come from our own research, from the experiences of others, and most especially from spirit guides and teachers, such as the MARKAS Energy, channeled by Gwen, who have helped us with this project. Please keep in mind that as we learn more about teleportation, and as the prevailing paradigm shifts, we are learning to bend and change "the rules." Experiencing the adventure of teleportation is a process, not a finished product!

Q: *Is it possible to teleport in the presence of others?*

A: You can teleport with other people in the same room as your point of departure, provided they are of like interest. At this time, because of prevailing beliefs, you can only go to a location that is either non-populated or appear in the presence of people who are experienced teleporters.

Q: *Can I take things along and could I leave them in different locations?*

A: You can take objects with you but you must bring them back when you return; otherwise, they would alter the reality of those in the area to which you teleported.

Q: *May I bring things back from a teleportation experience?*

A: You cannot take any object away from the area to which you teleport, again because it alters that reality. Even if you are given a gift while teleporting, you may not bring it back.

Q: *May I take my pet along?*

A: Initially, we thought pets could not even be in the same room with teleporters (unless the animals knew how to teleport). We've since learned that by explaining to your pets what is about to happen, you will comfort them thus you can depart and return in the presence of your animal friends.

Q: *What about time? Does it "stop" while I'm teleporting?*

A: Time "marches on;" we age physically during the time span of the teleportation experience, just as we would normally. If you are gone for twenty minutes, your watch will show a twenty minute difference when you return.

Q: *If something happens to my physical body while teleporting, will I retain the change when I return?*

A: You will bring back anything connected with the body even if it has changed in some way. For example, if you get a suntan while in the teleportation location, you will return with a suntanned body. Or, if you get ill while in the middle of a teleportation experience, you will bring the illness back as well. Physical body changes, then, do stay with you.

Q: *Will I always return to my original point of departure, and, will I always remember the experience?*

A: Most of the time you will remember the experience and you will return to your place of departure. There are times however, such as teleportation during sleep state, where you will not remember the experience. And, as we discussed earlier about "moving along a roadway" more quickly than normal, or the Atlantean boats skipping over great sections of water, you can sometimes "speed-forward," in a teleportation sense.

Q: *May I take a tape recorder or camera to help me remember the places I visit?*

A: Not at this point of time in the process. You cannot, in any way, record the experience while you are at the teleportation location, either by tape, film or writing the experience down on paper. This is because it would affect both realities, your point of origin and your destination site. After the teleportation experience, you must rely on your memory. We suggest you keep a notebook handy to quickly record the experience upon your return.

Q: *Can I teleport in a group, with my friends who are also learning to teleport?*

A: Yes, you can teleport in groups as long as you all have a common agreement concerning the destination of the teleportation. In the beginning, you may only see part of your friends at the designated destination. For example, you may see an arm, or a bit of shoe or just hear a familiar voice say one or two words. Don't be alarmed, the picture becomes more complete with practice!

Q: *You explained earlier that we may not do any thing (such as leave things behind), that would disrupt the reality of the place we've landed. But what about footprints left in soft sand or wet grass? Would they change the reality?*

A: When you teleport your vibration is altered. It is not always altered at the 100% level. At times you will leave part of your energy in your home and part of it travels to, say, Stonehenge. What percentage you dematerialize and then materialize depends on several factors. If your footprints are going to cause a disruption, a cosmic system of checks and balances takes over. You, the teleporter, will think you're over there, trampling the grass, moving around. You will be there, but only part of your energy will actually materialize in that location!

Q: *What percentage of you needs to teleport in order to actually leave footprints?*

A: It depends on where you go. Different places on the planet have different densities. For Stonehenge, in order for you to make a mark, you would need to be there at least 60%. It rains a lot there so to make a more lasting imprint you would need to be there upwards to 80 to 85%. This has to do with the energies that are in the ground and gravitational pull. It has nothing to do with your own body weight, it only has to do with the percentage that teleports.

Q: *What percentage needs to materialize in order for others to see you?*

A: To be a passing glance to others, at least 60% of you must teleport. To be fully seen, the percentage is greater, at least 80 to 85%. Have you ever seen something or someone just out of the corner of your eye? You blink, or spin around for a better look, and poof! Nothing. Perhaps you are noticing just a bit of someone teleporting in for a visit!

Q: *Is it possible to teleport to underwater locations? If so, how does the body handle a lack of oxygen?*

A: Again, it has to do with percentages. You can go underwater, or to other environments such as the tops of very high mountains, or even into space. Your physical body can handle a teleportation experience with approximately 10 to 50% of your energy teleporting. Anymore than 50% and you'll have to deal with weightier issues (sorry about the pun!). At this stage of human development, we need breathing apparatus, our lungs, and while we are rapidly developing for Fourth Dimensional reality, we are not there completely — yet. So at this point, while we can travel to locations underwater etc., we cannot materialize fully. You will have a legitimate teleportation experience, but with some physical restrictions. As our bodies evolve, this will be less and less of a difficulty.

Q: ***What if someone asks for some kind of physical demonstration or "proof" of teleportation - what do you do then?***

A: Teleportation is not a parlor game. If you're trying to use it to prove something to someone, you're going to create a disappointment. Teleportation is not about proving anything, it's about the transformation of one's energy. If you attempt to have concrete proof of something that defies the current paradigm, then you're going to have to spend a lot of time doing things the way present science can understand. You may never be able to prove it to everyone because there are certain individuals who have based their life's work on a certain framework. No matter what you do, you will not shift the understanding of some people. At a certain point, people who do not wish to teleport, or to even acknowledge it, will dig in their heels and will stop listening. You could teleport from one side of the parking lot to the next, a hundred times and still there are individuals who would consider the act a grand trick of illusion. As MARKAS says,

"There are beings on this planet who will never, never, have a teleportation experience. They're not here for that. It's not for all beings. And some of those beings who are never going to have a teleportation experience are the ones who will ask for the most proof! It will be like trying to explain something in Greek to someone who doesn't know the language and hasn't been to Greece. It will be very difficult. You will be spinning your wheels and running in circles. So if someone comes in and is very skeptical and very cynical and is malicious in their questioning, you may just wish to stop the game."

Provide the information to those who ask. But getting into the proving game, is, in our opinion, wasted energy. Use your energy instead to develop your skills in teleportation!

Q: ***I think I've had a teleportation experience. Is there a way I can share my experience with others?***

A: Yes! We are currently assembling a collection of experiences shared by our students and others. We intend to publish this collection in our next book. If you are interested in sharing your experiences, or if you have further questions about teleportation, please write us at the address below. We look forward to hearing from you!

Teleportation!

Words of Wizdom International, Inc.
P.O. Box 700830
San Antonio, Texas 78270

***Round and round we go,
and where we stop, nobody knows ...***

Chapter Ten

FULL CIRCLE: THE END IS REALLY JUST THE BEGINNING

It's all in the mind, you know.

Ringo Starr

*You are limited only by
your understanding of freedom.
Fly!*

Dreams of Splendor Dream Package

When we learn something new, when we expand our awareness, it is only natural to want to share this new knowledge with those we care about. In the beginning of this book, we discussed the motivation and inspiration for Jonathan Livingston Seagull in learning to fly for the pure joy of flight. After his meeting with Chiang, he decided to share his love of flying — *accelerated flying* — with other gulls. But first he needed to learn it, and earn it, by going it alone. And he did, successfully! That is when he returned to teach others.

Now the time had come to take the next step, to move on to the next level of his own development. Realizing this, Jonathan needed to choose his replacement as teacher, for new students need instruction! He had in mind a gull named Fletch, and he dangled the "carrot" of opportunity in front of him.

But Fletch resisted: he didn't feel qualified and, the truth was, he didn't want Jonathan to go away. Sometimes we need a little "push" to get us motivated for new opportunities, and so Jonathan, recognizing this, gave him the following insight, a gift of universal wisdom in the form of words of encouragement:

> *"Don't believe what your eyes are telling you... Look with your understanding, find out what you already know, and you'll see the way to fly."*[21]

And with that, Jonathan dematerialized as Fletch watched in amazement... and began his journey into the next level of development! We wish the same for you!

Happy Traveling!

Endnotes

1 Bach, Richard. *Jonathan Livingston Seagull,*
  Avon Books, New York. 1973.

2 ibid. p.80

3 Spalding, Baird T. *Life and Teaching of the Masters of the*
  Far East: Volume 3, DeVorss & Co., CA. 1935, p. 46.

4 Klein, Eric. *The Crystal Stair: A Guide to the Ascension,*
  Oughten House, CA. 1992, p. 14.

5 Rosemary Ellen Guiley, ed. *Encyclopedia of Mystical and*
  Paranormal Experience, HarperSanFrancisco, CA. 1991,
  pp. 507-509.

6 ibid. pp. 607-609.

7 *The Miami Herald Sunday,* June 17, 1990, p.4-I
  Fred Tasker, Staff Writer.

8 Chopra, Deepak. *Ageless Body, Timeless Mind:*
  The Quantum Alternative to Growing Old ,
  Harmony Books, New York, 1993, p. 85.

9 Ferguson, Marilyn. *The Aquarian Conspiracy,*
  St. Martin's Press, New York, 1980, pp. 65-67.

10 Solt and Egan. *Imagine: John Lennon,*
  Macmillian, New York, 1987, p. 166.

11 Faus, Marian. Roe v. Wade: *The Untold Story of*
  the Landmark Supreme Court Decision That Made
  Abortion Legal, Macmillian Publishing Company,
  New York, 1988, pp. 297-298.

12 Gabor, Andrea. The Man Who Discovered Quality:
  How W. Edwards Deming Brought the Quality Revolution
  To America, Times Books - Random House, New York,
  1990, p. 9.

13 Hohler, Robert T. *I Touch the Future,*
  Random House, New York, 1987, pp. 256-260.

14 Lenard, Phillipp. *Great Men of Science,*
  Doubleday and Co., Inc. New York, 1933, pp.12-16.

15 ibid. p.18

16 Cary, Alice. *Rosa Parks* in *"Book Age,"*
  Scott's Books Publishing, Seattle, WA. 1995, p. 3.

17 Chopra, Deepak. *Ageless Body, Timeless Mind:*
  The Quantum Alternative to Growing Old ,
  Harmony Books, New York, 1993, pp. 84-85.

18 Dyer, Wayne. *Real Magic,* HarperCollins,
  New York, 1992, p. 158.

19 Lehrman, Fredric. *The Sacred Landscape,*
  Celestial Arts Publishing, Berkeley, CA. 1988, p. 23

20 *The Miami Herald Sunday,* June 17, 1990, p.4-I
  Fred Tasker, Staff Writer.

21 Bach, Richard. *Jonathan Livingston Seagull,*
  Avon Books, New York, 1973, p. 125.

APPENDIX I

Reprinted with permission from *The Miami Herald*

The Lore and Legend of Bimini,
by Fred Tasker, Herald Staff Writer

Bimini - Linda Q. Perrin, an Omaha charity fund-raiser in this life, re-members living three of her 30 previous lives on the continent of Atlantis. That was before 10,000 B.C., when she says the ancient land mass sank into the Atlantic Ocean half a mile north of this Bahamas island.

"I had gills in my shoulders," she says. "I could breathe under water."

Perrin's memories of those lives come most vividly when the energy, the "lemon light," courses up into her throat as she snorkels down over the Bimini Road, a long, flat-rock ocean-floor formation that looks eerily like a highway leading down to the Lost Continent.

Perrin is not alone in her belief that a wondrous civilization thrived here millennia before our own. Edgar Cayce, the famous "sleeping prophet," predicted in 1934 that Atlantis would be found in these waters. David Zink, a Cayce disciple, came to Bimini in 1974 and concluded that benevo-lent beings from the distant star system Pleiades came and helped the At-lanteans build a sacred temple here.

And last month another group of explorers came to conduct its own search. In a seven-day expedition, the Quest for Atlantis - 30 adventurers of vari-ous professions and varying degrees of belief or doubt - swam down to the Bimini Road, floated in the healing spring, inspected the mysterious shark mound, linked hands before a full moon to chant the universal mantra, "Ommm," and drew their own conclusions.

"It may not be Atlantis...then again, it might," said William Donado, a doctor of archaeology from Cal State-Fullerton. "I don't have any problem with aliens. I'm from California. We're a little more open-minded there."

The people of Bimini, meanwhile, smiled, took the questers' money for food, drink and lodging, and kept their own counsel.

"It's not for me to say," concluded Deacon Clarence Ellis of Bimini's Mount Zion Baptist Church.

Live and Let Live

Biminites are used to questers. They know their island is a mosquito on the face of America, buzzing just out of arm's reach 50 miles off Miami, a

121

natural haven for those who live by their own rules.

And they know that every century brings a new type of quester: 1600's British freebooters raiding the Spanish fleet; 1800's shipwreckers preying on fat merchant galleys; 20th Century fast boats running rum and cocaine; writers and disgraced politicians seeking respite, or, most recently, a presidential candidate monkeying around where he thought his secrets were safe.

This 9.5-square-mile triangle of islands packs more colorful history per square foot than anyplace else in The Bahamas.

The search for Atlantis, the ancient, fabled land of ivory-roofed golden palaces, ideal government and maybe even flying machines, has gone on since 300 B.C., when the Greek philosopher Plato wrote of it in his works *Critias* and *Timaeus*.

But the impetus for last month's exploration dates back only to 1934, when Edgar Cayce, seventh-grade dropout, stationery salesman, Sunday school teacher and much-heralded "sleeping prophet," went into one of his hypnotic trances and made a prediction: "The sunken portion of Atlantis...a portion of the temples, may yet be discovered under the slime of ages of sea water near what is known as Bimini, off the coast of Florida. Expect it in 1968 and 1969; not so far away."

Curious Discovery

In 1968 a Miami zoologist and amateur archaeologist named J. Manson Valentine went swimming in the gin-clear water a half-mile off Bimini's Paradise Point, looked down at the bottom 18 feet below, and discovered what today is called the "Bimini Road."

He saw hundreds of flat rocks, eight feet square and two feet thick, maybe 10 tons each, arranged not quite tongue-in-groove, but in a curiously regular pattern forming a half-mile-long, 100 yard wide reverse "J," running southwest to northeast.

Was it natural or man-made? Simple sediment or the road to Atlantis?

Most geologists called it natural. Then David D. Zink, a former U.S. Air Force Academy English professor intrigued with the origins of myths, arrived to study it in 1974.

Zink had a geologist analyze the stones, and determined that they were, indeed, sedimentary, but made of shells that don't occur naturally here. They must have been quarried elsewhere and placed here, he concluded. By Atlanteans.

Zink then departed radically from traditional archeological methods. He asked a Houston psychic named Carol Huffstickler to do a reading of the site. She astonished Zink by telling him the rocks were not a road, but fallen pillars of an ancient sacred temple. They were probably erected in about 28,000 B.C., she said. By Atlanteans.

She said the Atlanteans were aided by advanced, friendly beings from the star cluster Pleiades.

On a Quest

The story had a certain inner logic. Atlantis means "pertaining to Atlas," the ancient Greek god who supported the pillars holding apart heaven and earth. The most visible stars in the Pleiades cluster are called "The Seven Sisters," who, in Greek myth, are the seven daughters of Atlas.

That is what brought the Quest for Atlantis, organized by Joan Hanely of Tampa and Vanda Osmon of California, tour organizers and questers themselves. On a hot May morning recently, a dozen questers strapped on scuba gear and dived down over the road.

The rocks were stunning, lying in more-or-less regular patterns, covered in moss, with living coral sea fans waving in purple majesty at passing schools of jacks, grunts and angel fish.

Members of the Quest drew different conclusions.

"I can accept that it's natural, but there are some very odd things that suggest it might not be," says Doug Richards, a Ph.D. zoologist who is research director of the Cayce Foundation-funded Atlantic University in Virginia Beach, Va.

"Rocks on top of other rocks. You see so much stuff that's natural, and then you see that. You don't know what to think."

He isn't sure what to make of the psychics' pronouncements, Cayce's included.

"That's out of my realm entirely," said a more traditional archaeologist, Gypsy Graves, director of Fort Lauderdale's Museum of Archaeology. If she tried to report to a group of conservative archaeologists about the use of psychics, "they'd snicker, if they let you give the paper at all," she said.

There's no real evidence that the stones are part of Atlantis, Graves said. But she's intrigued enough that she wants to return next year with more sophisticated equipment. She regrets that lack of money and time has prevented a more professional probe of the Bimini Road site.

"They should look deeper," she said.

Graves' doubts didn't bother Hanley, the group leader.

"We don't know if this is Atlantis; we're here to see."

Theories Abound

The Atlantis questers' mental machinations interest Biminites only mildly.

"I think its Atlantis," says Bonefish Ben Francis, a Bimini fishing guide and shop owner. "I heard stories from the old people when I was a little boy that the [Bahamas] islands were once all one mass." But Francis has taken visitors out in his boat to dive over the Bimini Road for 20 years without ever going down to see it for himself.

"I'm not a diver. I'm a fisherman."

When the questers gathered at a Biminite friend's house that night, talk turned to other theories about the Bimini Road.

Zink, in his 1979 book, *The Ancient Stones Speak*, said the road is not an isolated phenomenon. He said it fits in a neat "planetary grid" with other mysterious megaliths, from the Great Pyramid in Giza to Ankor Wat to Stonehenge to the curious stone structures on Easter Island.

Zink believes many civilizations, separated widely in both history and geography, came to understand that the Earth's natural magnetic and electrical energy flows closer to the surface at certain places. At those sites, which girdle the Earth in a geodesic dome pattern, they built their sacred temples.

It also explains the "healing hole." Hidden beneath mangrove thickets on nearby East Bimini Island is a natural freshwater spring, very slightly radioactive, heavy in sulphur, which most doctors agree is good for bursitis and arthritis.

A group of questers had explored and floated in the spring that hot May day, hacking their way in with machetes and shooing away four small sharks who live there.

And they explored the "shark mound," a large, fish-shaped mound in the mangroves that archaeologist Graves hopes to study more next year. It might be natural, she said, or it might be an ancient burial mound.

Meditation Network

By 11 p.m. the full May moon was high in the eastern sky. And Osmon, who calls herself a "global networker," took the group outside for a Wesak Full Moon Meditation. It was part of a worldwide network of such meditations taking place at many of the Earth's megalithic sites, but focused on a central festival in a mountain valley in Tibet.

The Bimini group sat cross-legged on a dock facing the bright, yellow moon. Waves washed gently against the dock. Lines slapped quietly against masts of sailboats in the marina. The feeling was gentle, comradely. Osmon didn't insist on dogma."Let your prayers go on the wind. Whatever feels comfortable. Let us meditate together focusing on the moon and our global participation." The group formed a circle, holding hands. In the middle, Osmon handed out candles, poured water from one vessel into another and arranged her crystals. "This is a healing circle," she said. Meditators lifted their held hands over their heads and, for 30 seconds, chanted the mantra: "Ommmmmmm!" It ended with long, warm hugs.

And Deacon Ellis's benediction: "To each his own."

Mystical Atlantis

Plato: The Greek philosopher couldn't have known he was setting off a 2,300-year debate when, in 300 B.C., he first mentioned Atlantis in his works, *Critias* and *Timaeus*. He described a huge island, existing in about 10,000 B.C., with an ideal government and advanced agriculture, an elaborate system of canals and bridges, opulent temples with ceilings of ivory and roofs of gold. Ruled by Poseidon (Neptune) and his 10 sons, including Atlas, the kingdom threatened to overwhelm Europe. Then its people grew corrupt, and the island was violently destroyed by volcanoes.

Early scholars took the story literally and believed Atlantis sank in the Atlantic Ocean near the Straits of Gibraltar. Most today believe Plato meant the story as an allegory for human potential and sins, and believe that the story of Plato's Atlantis - as well as the flood that inspired the story of Noah in the Bible - arose from the volcanic destruction of Thira, an island 100 miles off Greece in the Aegean Sea, in 1470 B.C.

Edgar Cayce: The seventh-grade-dropout-turned-'sleeping prophet' (1877-1945) believed he could diagnose illness, interpret dreams, read the past and foretell the future in a hypnotic trance. It was in exploring his subjects' past lives that Cayce discovered Atlantis, a topic that came to make up 30 percent of Cayce's life's readings.

His concept was even more wondrous, if a bit fuzzier, than Plato's. He believed Atlantis was an island near Bimini where an advanced civilization peaked in 50,000 B.C. and was destroyed in 10,000 B.C. By understanding the Earth's fundamental electrical and gravitational forces, Atlanteans built "boats" that flew by something akin to teleportation. The same forces helped Atlanteans lift mammoth stones to build splendid temples. The end began when the Atlanteans became corrupt and developed the "fire stone," a "terrible mighty crystal" of incredible force. It was to be for good, to control the "great animals overrunning the Earth." But somehow its rays "set in motion the fires in the inner portions of the earth." And volcanoes destroyed Atlantis.

125

ABOUT THE AUTHORS

Gwen Totterdale, Ph.D., M.B.A.,C.P.A., is a metaphysical counselor, researcher and author. She has an extensive background in business and accounting, having taught on the accounting faculty at several universities. In 1986, she turned her attention to the field of metaphysics and in 1988 began conducting seminars and private sessions on metaphysical philosophies, intuition, spirit communication, table tipping and, in recent years, telepathy, teleportation and aura photography. She is the trance channel for the Markas Energy.

In 1989 Dr. Totterdale began to develop global, environmental tours, the result of a deep love for the ocean and desire for a healthier planet. Beyond these specialty tours, which include swimming with dolphins and discovering spiritual energies in different cultures, she is producing feature videos on dolphin communication and the dolphin/human connection. She makes her home in Hawaii.

Jessica Severn, Ph.D. is currently the Director of a private business college on the west coast of the United States. She holds a Doctorate in Communication and has been a professor and administrator in higher education for the past 20 years. Her interest in metaphysics began in childhood as she and her father spent hours discussing auras, time/space travel, spirit guides and the worlds beyond the third dimension. Dr. Severn is an avid traveler and an accomplished sailor. She divides her time between the shimmering blues of the Caribbean and the deep forest greens of the Pacific Northwest.

If you would like more information or a brochure on:

Dolphin Discovery World Tours
Lancelot's Desire Metaphysical Journeys
Channeling Sessions with Markas
Markas Audiotapes
Aura Photography

please contact:

Gwen Totterdale, Ph.D.
Lancelot's Desire
P.O. Box 990
Waimanalo, HI 96795

Phone/Fax: U.S. & Canada 1-800-888-3657
International   (808) 259-8530

To all of my companions,
physical and nonphysical,
who light my path daily.

And to my dad, with love.

G.T. 1995

To the curious,
the adventurous
and the eternally young at heart.
And to all those who, like the Fool in the ancient Tarot,
leap into the unknown,
willing to risk the security of familiarity
for the joy of something new.

And to a dear old friend, William James.

J.S. 1995

Special Thanks To:

Tracy O'Reilly Kohlrautz
for her courage and her willingness to take risks
— in life and in business.

Joe H. Hostatler for his assistance and research.

The many who have provided moments of inspiration,
insight, humor and wisdom as this book was taking form.

Our students and fellow travelers
for their insights and experiences.

As Spirit notes:

Blending space and time,
Universal ideas become your creation.

Dreams of Splendor Dream Package

Thank you for the ideas!